Vectors of Desire

Vectors of Desire

Terry Rodgers' Vision of the American Millennial Moment

Jim Zimmerman

iUniverse, Inc.
New York Lincoln Shanghai

Vectors of Desire
Terry Rodgers' Vision of the American Millennial Moment

iUniverse, Inc.

For information address:
iUniverse, Inc.
2021 Pine Lake Road, Suite 100
Lincoln, NE 68512
www.iuniverse.com

A Standing Watch Book
Amsterdam · Milan · New York · Gravesend
standingwatch@aol.com

Cover: *Second Sight* (2004, 63" x 80", detail)

To see these paintings in color and more visit **www.terryrodgers.com**.

Cover Design: Estelle Rodgers and Chip Brown

ISBN: 0-595-32884-9

Printed in the United States of America

Contents

Illustrations

Preface

The work of the American realist painter Terry Rodgers documents and maps the sources, forces, directions, and implications of desire and its counterpart, constraint, in the late twentieth and early twenty-first centuries, particularly in America, but also, and increasingly, throughout the sophisticated, urbanized, technologically-driven world. Desire is the basis of our being and doing, and it is also the basis for commotion, confusion, and endless, often unfortunate, complication. Rodgers employs what he calls "an architecture of vectors" to submerge us in present moments replete with every challenge and conundrum of contemporary human experience. He shows us fascinating faces and figures in puzzling, unreadable situations. We are thrust into the vortex of clashing self-consciousnesses and challenged to read them, goaded almost, to the point where we can't help trying to read ourselves. These extravagantly painted human figures never precisely indicate but definitely do suggest all the peculiar varieties of human feeling, thought, and action. And they evoke the enduring questions that have perennially troubled and inspired philosophers as well as artists and ordinary people. What are these people thinking and doing with their lives? What are they intending and fearing? What is being said or shown of human life and experience, about specific, exotic sub-cultures, and about a whole civilization? In the reluctant, intensely private self-recognition we finally feel, what do we discover about the high-profile public people we've become?

Desire was the defining subject of the America of the late twentieth century. It was explored and celebrated in every medium. But how do you paint desire? How do you capture its richness, power, complexity, and meaning? How do you represent on canvas the emotional, psychological, and moral dynamics of human beings who have been persuaded that they can have whatever they want? This monograph almost accidentally answers those questions in the process of considering more than fifty major oil paintings made by Rodgers between 1990 and 2005. In the absence of a retrospective of the artist's work at this writing, the following discussion is intended to offer an understanding of the scope, richness, and complexity of the artist's production over the past fifteen years. Because most of the paintings are in the hands of private collectors, the best way to get to know them is through the artist's website (www.terryrodgers.com), where all of the images reproduced here in black and white are available in color. For the student of Rodgers, what follows can be seen as a supplement to the website.

I've had a unique opportunity to get to know the artist and his work. In the past two years, during the course of the research for this monograph, I've seen firsthand all but two of the paintings discussed below (in shows, in the artist's studio, or in his home) and conducted interviews with curators, gallery owners, critics, and collectors, as well as many with the artist himself. In addition to seeing every painting made for the shows in Milan, New York, Los Angeles, Atlanta, Columbus, Chicago, and Amsterdam (as well as subsequently attending the Milan, New York, and Atlanta shows), I've also had the opportunity to see dozens of Rodgers' works in various styles and media dating back to the 1970's. Finally, I've been a witness to his gradual elaboration of the "party metaphor"—incrementally evolved via hundreds of models, props, and design experiments—as a way of exploring American culture.

In addition to his technical powers, Rodgers is preternaturally attuned to the sea changes and tidal rhythms of American culture, and how the endlessly breaking waves of art crash onto the shores of commerce, where the latest manifestations of fashion, design, advertising, and cinema splash into being. This modest monograph is significant simply because it takes the first step toward filling a vacuum; it brings attention to the career of an artist who is in the midst of a prodigiously productive period and is on the verge of attracting the critical notice he deserves, and will certainly soon command, owing to his irresistible subject matter, his remarkable technical accomplishment, and his overall vision of painting and culture. I hope the reader will bear with me in my enthusiasm for Rodgers and forgive any apparent excesses when, after seeing so much of his oeuvre, speaking with him at such length, and witnessing him at work in his studio on so many occasions, I am tempted to paraphrase Huysmans on Degas and say that, these days, I sometimes feel that no one else knows how to paint.

Introduction

On a humid June morning in Columbus, Ohio, I drove a few blocks out of the downtown area and entered the neighborhood of Terry Rodgers' studio. Among the warehouses, bars, and parking lots, I felt as if I'd passed into an America of the mid-twentieth century that still existed in a faded, forlorn, dilapidated kind of way. A coal train passed overhead as I arrived at the unremarkable industrial building where Rodgers' van was parked at a loading dock.

Once inside, I was confronted with a spectacular new painting, almost six feet high and over eight feet long, a sensational accomplishment that might well be his masterpiece, with a dozen or more figures creating vectoral magic and a woven complexity that invites the eye to roam quite contentedly for half an hour. (Not until the next day would Rodgers come to a decision about the name of the painting he had nearly completed; he called it *Shades of Olympus*.) Rodgers, delighted that the air-conditioning had been restored in the building, was getting close to finishing the picture, which lacked a hand here, a shirt there, a chair somewhere else, and perhaps a little perspectival correction regarding the way the floor disappeared beneath a figure on its way to the fireplace one can barely glimpse between two other figures. For an hour, I looked at the new work and listened to Rodgers talk about it. He spoke of the churning, roiling excitement of the right-hand side of the painting as contrasted with the comparative calm of the left side, where a figure very like Paris Hilton serenely sported lingerie in a pose somewhere between dancer and mannequin.

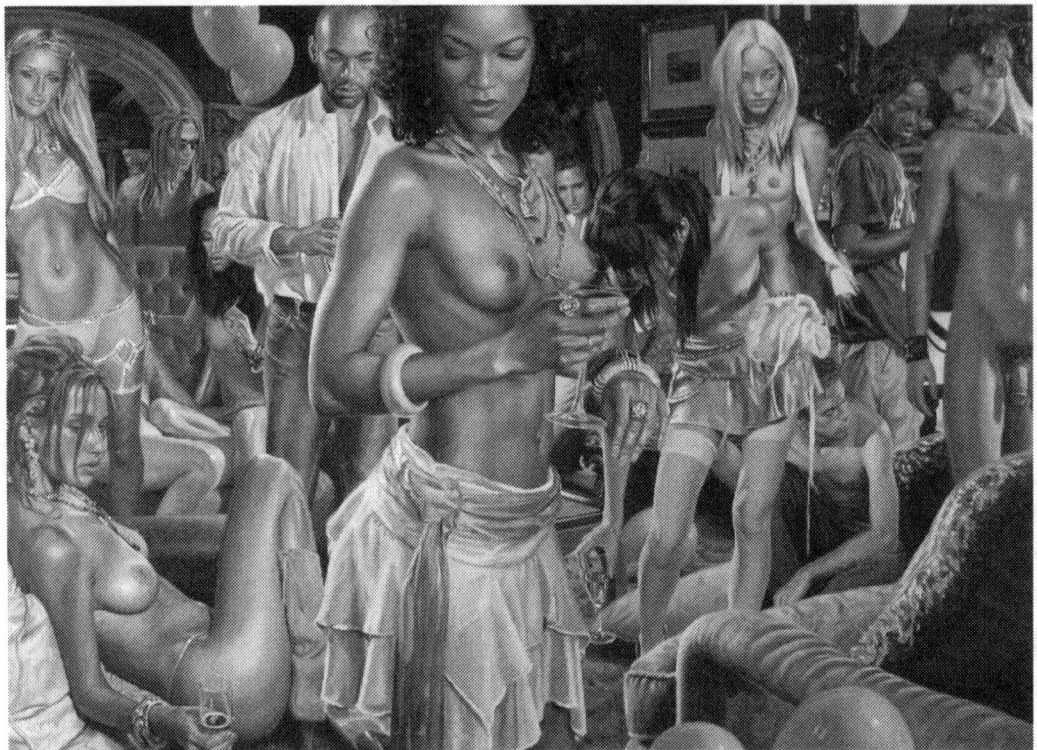

Fig. 1. *Shades of Olympus* (2004, 70 ½" x 99")

We discussed the packaging of the female body in Western culture and the stunning difference regarding the male—how underwear and breasts and even genitalia are so presented and elaborated and discussed on the one hand, and how strikingly rare it is to see male genitalia, so-called full frontal male nudity, as Rodgers shows us in the case of *Shades of Olympus*. We talked about the shock of seeing "realistic" scenes and figures painted with depth and dimensionality, and how unprepared we are now to take them in, as opposed to our complacent acceptance of a Reubens, as if the latter is quaint and charming, and not really about a living person.

As if the notion of "a living person" is so certain and knowable at any time in history. As if perception, personality, character, and even anatomy itself are constants. As if we haven't recognized the complexity of sensing the self in others and the otherness of the self. Rodgers is delighted by the abstractions that we treat as solid and substantial in our daily lives, the flimsy notions that we rely upon as if they were beyond doubt. As if we don't realize that even light is fickle, that the whole universe is running away from itself, and that we fail to solve our problems at every level, whether they involve nursing homes or war or traffic.

In the past decade-and-a-half, by devoting himself to large oil paintings depicting the American cultural present, Rodgers has compiled a remarkable record of the millennial moment in American culture and developed a painterly-realist technique that renders human behavior in gorgeous large canvases. In exhibits in the United States and in Europe, Rodgers has shown works that present a record of American preoccupations while loosening and expanding his painterly techniques to create a visual feast. Critics began to take note of Rodgers in the late Nineties, and by the turn of the new century some observers noted a particular quality to the content and form of the paintings. Regarding the nine works in the 2002 Fay Gold Gallery show, Lilly Wei, in her catalogue essay, remarked on the "unrequited, unidentified, unplaceable desire" (*Terry Rodgers*, Fay Gold Gallery, 2002). This is a brilliant insight into the subject matter and technique of a painter who has set out to show us contemporary life through his restless brushes, extravagant color sense, and complex designs.

In the first years of the new millennium, Rodgers continues to find new ways to celebrate painterly and traditional techniques in a fusion of realist painting that is aesthetically and intellectually rewarding. Rodgers is at the height of his creative powers, or near it, at this writing. His energy and vision are so all-consuming that he can spend seven days a week in his studio, and then come home late at night to make dinner with his wife, only to eagerly turn to his computer to review photographs of models and explore design concepts for future paintings. The talent and the ambition of the painter are noteworthy, and the sheer joy in creation is extraordinary. He appears insatiable in his own appetite for making pictures. He is thriving in an intellectual, spiritual, and artistic space that is all his own, with no thought of finally achieving an end. He paints out of a seemingly inexhaustible desire to see what he can make. "My subject is the limitless human complexity that can never really be penetrated," he says.

Rodgers' gorgeous and disturbing work typically elicits instantaneous reactions from viewers: either an amused introspection or a defensive dismissal impelled by the rebellious refusal to participate. This is partly because Rodgers is expert at presenting an ever-so-slightly-"other"-ness and partly because he is obviously employing the mischief of seduction. We are accustomed, trained really (as a matter of daily self-defense), to exert intellectual and moral resistance to anything that smacks of unreconstructed seduction. We are ready to resist, as if the threat posed by the paintings attacks both our moral and our intellectual view of the world we live in. The characteristic reaction to these figurative works is therefore oddly akin to the kind of reactions some viewers have to abstract, conceptual, and performance art works. We catch ourselves wondering, "What could this have to do with me? What does it mean?" But instead of interpreting lines, shapes, patterns, ideas, and actions divorced from human faces, we are forced to ask, "To what extent do these finely-rendered realist representations of human life have anything to say about the way I am living my own life?" Some viewers quickly reject the paintings as voyeuristic, superficial, or trivial. The patient, observant, thoughtful viewer, however, is presently seduced just as much by Rodgers' profound comments and searing insights into our affinities, aspirations, associations, attitudes, and values as they are by his technical brilliance. My argument is that this painter presents us with substantive observations, comments, insights—even revelations—about, as Anthony Trollope put it, "the way we live now," and he does this even as he extends the technical and theoretical dialogue about abstraction, realism, tradition, technique, and meaning in art.

Rodgers obviously paints in the humanist-liberal-realist tradition that seems (when we react with the standard, contemporary reflex) old-fashioned, obsolete, worn-out, and dead-end. But because he paints in the postmodern period, we are also attuned to the tricks and tropes and playfulness, the allusions and inclusions and exclusions. He has a masterly capacity to employ and reproduce the phenomena of light and color in stunning ways. Reflection, refraction, magnification, distortion, shadow, and just plain old exaggeration for effect are treats that await the viewer in every work. But above and beyond his skill with a brush and his eye for tone, texture, and detail, he observes and comments on our methods of communication and our ways of being. There are frequent telephones, newspapers and magazines, one memorable laptop computer (but no larger computers or television sets); an abundance of cinematic and fashion elements; and ubiquitous and endlessly varied facial expressions, gestures, postures, and body language. More importantly, he captures people at unmasked, exposed moments in the midst of an impossibly distractive, interruptive, and disorienting world. And he presents human figures in the midst of subtle movements that explode with vectors indicating—and inviting us to see—the meaningful dynamic qualities of the cultural present, the web of forces almost invisibly (and definitely irresistibly) at work on us, and particularly on young people emerging from the questionable protection of their childhood settings.

We see gorgeous faces and voluptuous figures, with exquisitely rendered eyes, lips, ears, fingers, breasts, bellies, and legs, not to mention the lavish settings they inhabit and the splendid, exotic objects that surround them, apparently encroaching upon their consciousness and shaping their behavior. There is an unmistakable sense of entrapment amid riches, of a disorientation that stems from too many desires, too many forces pulling them in too many directions, and simply too much stuff. In fact, there is a sense in which Rodgers paints characters who wish for freedom from desire.

They are trapped in a "What have you done (or acquired) lately?" kind of world in which satisfaction is always just beyond our reach. It is a world unmistakably brought to life in Rodgers' work, a densely materialistic environment that we can gaze on and marvel at, and a world that then seems to watch us, as if there is a palpable give-and-take, a distinct dialogue, between the painted image and our self-conscious assimilation of it. Rodgers' paintings can be an affront, a rebuke, a shock, a spectacle, or a revelation to us, but rarely a consolation.

Taken as a whole, however, Rodgers' work points to a "moment" in which human beings might find themselves, for better or worse. The Rodgerian moment is not necessarily about personal revelation or even significance. It's about, for lack of better words and phrases, what we call reality, actual experience, and the pure awareness of being. Classical rhetorical theory offers us a model for the moment Rodgers seems drawn to: the notion of stasis, or the stopping-point. Aristotle, Quintilian, Cicero, and Vico contributed to the tradition of asking provocative and productive, though disarmingly fundamental questions about typical human situations, and Rodgers' paintings echo and reinforce those questions with their vivid depictions of paradoxical complexity in social settings. "Did something happen?" is one of the classic philosophic, rhetorical, and forensic questions. Or, in the case of many of Rodgers' works, "Is something about to happen?" And—whether it has happened or is about to—"Is harm involved? If so, what kind of harm? Is someone guilty? Or does someone just feel guilty? Or if they don't, should they? And why?" Ultimately, beyond guilt or innocence, there is the question of basic identity: who these people are, how they are put together in their own heads, and who I am among all of them and all of this. Who are we, enmeshed in an advanced culture that shields us from our animal essence—our unavoidable, unrefinable, unrelenting instincts and inclinations—and yet uses that to lure us into the next trap?

Rodgers has called his paintings "investigations." Through the use of gestural dynamics, with vectors pointing in multiple directions, adding up one way and canceling each other out in another way, the artist directs our attention to certain aspects of experience and, in particular, American culture, whatever that happens to be this season. Paradoxically, his active compositions both suggest the swirl of thought, feeling, and behavior even as they put the moment (and the culture itself) on hold. By fixing everything in a frozen moment of obvious in-between-ness, he is able to make the case that what we think of as a broad, stable system is in fact a congeries of unrecognized and often unidentifiable systems in such rapid motion, and undergoing such rapid evolution, that none of us can completely perceive all that is going on, much less understand it. Watching television and movies and using the Internet is exhausting and unsatisfying as simple entertainment but even more so if one is trying to understand the culture. There is simply too much culture—or too many cultures. No one can assimilate it, make simple sense of it, or convincingly articulate a coherent synthesis of its nature or significance. But somehow, in painting after painting, Rodgers has managed to embed the dynamics of American culture in his work, and thus to point us toward possible interpretations, toward a heightened sense of awareness and a greater emphasis on meaning. He has energetically lived in the midst of the culture he paints—participated in it, observed it, analyzed it, processed it—and his recent body of work gives us a unified if still somewhat mysterious vision of where things stand in the America of this protracted, slow-motion millennial moment. Even more importantly, he sees individual people in the culture as they are at any given instant, and he shows them to us in dramatic fashion, allowing us to add it up ourselves, one eye, one finger, one hand, one arm, one shoulder, one forehead, or one breast at a time. We think that we know what most parts of the human anatomy connote, but in our time the fragments of skin (or, in certain paintings, the waves of skin) seem to be developing new connotations, and something as familiarly exciting as nudity isn't exactly what it used to be. This nakedness is something else, something evolving and ever newer, and Rodgers lets us decide for ourselves what human creatures living unfettered (and so close to their skin) might next become.

Despite the obvious fact that Rodgers' recent work is unquestionably in the realist tradition and seems to offer easy accessibility to the viewer, much of it recalls Gertrude's Stein's statement about daunting literary technique: "…a long complicated sentence should force itself upon you, make yourself know yourself knowing it" (*Lectures in America* 221). Coming face-to-face with a Rodgers canvas that measures five to seven feet by eight to twelve feet and includes a dozen or more characters frozen in unreadable postures, with (at first glance) affectless expressions, we do in fact come to know ourselves knowing it. There is no other way. It takes time to absorb even a fraction of what is there, and it takes a rich self-conscious awareness to find all of the playful touches and hide-and-seek details. And to read the subtle facial expressions requires both patience and imagination; it demands that we stop and consider the way the human face works when in its most private mode. In addition to his brilliant technical skill and dazzling settings and figures, Rodgers makes us self-conscious about viewing realistic painting, about the machinery of making meaning, and about our place in his vision of the American millennial moment. Beyond that, he challenges our own personal vision to account for the particular factors he emphasizes. How does all of this add up as far as we are concerned?

Rodgers uses multiple approaches to present his ideas. In addition to the social commentary and brilliantly-rendered realism of Rodgers' work (and allowing for the ever-present invitation to sniff out the hint of a narrative), we also notice multiple elements of symbolism and even allegory. Paintings with titles like *Shades of Olympus* and *The Labyrinth* certainly invite us to make large-scale metaphoric and mythic connections. But Rodgers is less interested in metaphorical freight than in the dazzling details he foregrounds and their more camouflaged counterparts. He is, above all else, a painter who celebrates color, light, the human figure, and the painterly things a brush— sometimes a very small one, sometimes a large one—can do on a linen surface. Many of his works have painterly qualities that can be as rewarding to study as the figures themselves. But all of his paintings lead us back into our own lives, our stasis, our momentum, our direction, and our baffled and often inscrutable desire. Poet Linda Pastan observes, "What we want/is never simple./We move among the things/we thought we wanted…"("What We Want"). When material wants are easily satisfied, what we lack becomes a mystery, and then perhaps a quest, until it is practically petrified into a religion.

In the America that Rodgers investigates, every enigma and unanswered question in the mystery-quest of life is subsumed under the secular faith in "freedom and democracy." There is a mytho-historical habit of looking to America for these vague entities, and American leaders often consider themselves proprietors, packagers, and exporters of these ideals, even as individuals in America ask themselves if they really feel free, and if this American myth is working for them. "We confuse 'freedom' with 'the freedom to have,'" as Rodgers puts it. "We want things, and we want people, and we want them to do what we want them to do." Rodgers shows us people "like us" in his pictures, even if they don't superficially resemble us. Like them, we tend to associate the idea of our own freedom with someone who will liberate us from ourselves: from responsibility, habit, obligation, repetition. But instead of liberating us, these people end up being our acquisitions, accomplishments, or trophies. By "having" them, we make ourselves more interesting and more individual, and we "express ourselves." (When we can't have them, we tend to feel rejected and defeated.) To express oneself fully is to be "unique," but in a culture bursting at the seams with unique people, uniqueness becomes at best a posture, and at worst a compulsion. The competition to be different is crushing, and the idea of "being oneself" in the face of the frenetically generated new influences, trends, fads, and other distractions seems like a joke.

Frequently, in the world Rodgers paints, it appears that personal freedom lies outside the space the preoccupied figures inhabit. In fact, they might be seen to be imagining a whole new place, a completely different world, where they could become themselves. The irony is that "the idea of America" is a golden state of grace for many people around the world. But if you're already in America, already a full-fledged American citizen, where do you turn? For Americans east of the Mississippi, California is the typical dream destination, but Alaska and Hawaii are also often invoked; or perhaps even some place other than America, because to be an American expatriate, to actually turn one's back on America, is to be doubly romantic about the American Dream. If a new place isn't possible, one re-makes the old person or place in a new image, or overlays an idea that promises the particular kind of personal freedom we know we should have been enjoying all along. When will "The Dream" begin for us? In order to actualize our potential freedom, we try products, services, places, relationships, and gurus. Popular music often represents a great promise of freedom to dependent, unenfranchised youth and the partially-enfranchised poor. (Martin Luther King, Jr.'s brilliantly nebulous re-invention of The American Dream continues to fuel desire, however vaguely.) Sometimes, especially among the well-off and well-educated, art holds out the promise of true freedom. But if Rodgers' paintings are to help us find freedom, we've got considerable work to do. We have to understand what it is we desire.

In his major paintings since 1990, Rodgers has put a mirror to American desires, including desires of and for "America" and all it represents, individually, collectively, culturally, nationally, globally. The idea of "America" cannot be separated from the concepts, excessive (and obesity-inducing) standards, and mindless expectations of food in abundance, entertainment every waking moment, impeccable dental care, touch-or-click temperature control, the anti-animalistic subtlety of quietly effective plumbing, and the very best of shiny high-tech appliances, and many of them. These are all assumed and obviously present, if largely out of sight, in the world of Rodgers' paintings. Also, there is abundance in general, comfort that in most quarters and eras would be considered luxury, opportunity that verges on the fantastic, as well as endless, constant, ubiquitous stimulation. There is, in short, everything that any of us could want, except steady, reliable, warm human connection, the *ne plus ultra* that is also the fundamental human building block of a life worth living. "Love," of course, is an occupational hazard for the practicing super-consumer; when one can survey the menu of men and women presented in the media, love is problematic, in terms of the kind of committed constancy that involves solid, sincere, welcome bonds. The love we see presented by Rodgers is a problem, a lack, a possibility, a hope, a fantasy, or a puzzle. The lure of love—the continual awareness of its being out there somewhere—is quite possibly even a burden. Rodgers' paintings seem to push us away because it is very easy not to like what they show us, one situation after another in which the chief actors are as likely to look foolish as they are to look cool. We are called upon to make an effort to judge or connect with the figures in each painting—and, by extension, to judge or connect with the other people in the gallery, and then passersby in the street, and, ultimately, those intimate strangers who populate our private lives.

Once we submit ourselves fully to a Rodgers painting, the first thing we notice, especially about many of the recent large oils, is the way that multiple figures are stopped in time, awkwardly, as if spatially as well as chronologically interrupted; they appear disconnected from each other and physically at odds with their environment, but they also appear to be listening. (Each painting makes us wonder about the aural environment.) Frequently, in gallery settings, with several large Rodgers' canvases in the same space, viewers say they are overwhelmed with the size, number, undress, and unease of the figures. But the size, in particular, is also an invitation to engagement. And, once engaged, we are hard-pressed to insist that these paintings have nothing to do with our thoughts, our values, and our experiences. What Rodgers records, in heightened and ironic fashion, is a version of what many Americans live every day: unparalleled ease and opulence, overwhelming stimulation, and a sophistication of styles that is all too often under-appreciated. Elaborately designed and executed clothing, jewelry, hair, make-up, furniture, architecture, art, and even posture and gesture are a given of contemporary culture. In terms of material wealth, many Americans live like kings and queens, but they are a new class of commonplace royalty forever seeking refuge, forever on the run, or waiting, then hurrying and worrying again, stomachs churning with the mix of anxiety and rich food, like royal refugees, always on the move or at least restlessly fretting. The characters Rodgers creates are model citizens in an ever-expanding empire of style. They struggle to find themselves in the chaos of a mélange of low, middle, and high culture. Whether they are stuck in traffic, waiting for an elevator, shopping at the supermarket, or surfing the Internet, the thought of their own peculiar identity and its significance is never far from their worried minds. Rodgers is an observer of all of this; he's a gregarious presence everywhere he goes, full of questions, but with an uncanny ability to provoke and then to listen. Above all, to see.

Wherever he travels, Rodgers plunges into the life of the streets. But he also immerses himself in art and literature, and revels in opera and fashion, because he sees these high culture forms as the apotheosis of generations of popular culture—forms that continue to be alive to change and surprise. In the realm of painting in particular, Rodgers especially admires the techniques of Velasquez, Romney, Sargent, and Zorn. He returns to works by these artists to study their use of paint and their achievement of what he elliptically calls "the abstraction of realism." Among the many painters whose subject matter and attitude interest him, once again the name of Velasquez comes first to his lips, followed by Toulouse-Lautrec, Degas, Beckman, Grosz, Lucien Freud, Fischl, Richter, and Salle. He sees the work of many of the painters on this second list as "emotionally real…without the fine brushwork," and their works as achievements that "do not look like something but communicate it anyway." With Richter and Salle, in particular, Rodgers delights in their "looking at 'looking at'."

One collector of Rodgers' work, having first encountered it in a Miami show, said, "Your works struck me on many levels from the brilliance of your composition, reminiscent of Renoir's compositions and Caravaggio's perspective, to Manet's brushstrokes. You are the modern

Baudelarian *flaneur*, the ultimate voyeur of modern life. Your paintings are gripping, annoying, startling, and beautiful all at once, the marks of classic work."

Rodgers, as he plots the paths of desire into the third millennium of the Christian era, sees saints and martyrs and satyrs and hermits living among us, apparently civilized, socialized, and homogenized. But the evidence is there in his paintings that we are the same primitive creatures who existed before fashion and architecture and ornament and ego took on lives of their own. We are hunting and being hunted; we are wanting and being wanted; and we are awash in a universe of forces that we cannot fully understand, many of which originate in our own wild psyches, but most of which we are born into, uncomprehendingly submerged in from birth.

1. The Big Picture

"The marvelous beauty and the temptation are always there,
yet all of that does nothing but beg the bigger questions."
—Terry Rodgers

Rodgers is the painter of the promise, the fantastic human promise that remains unrealized. Often using recognizably, even uniquely American elements, Rodgers plays with particular variations of the mythic American Dream to get at his larger project, which is concerned with humanity, individuality, personality, identity, and character. He investigates the meaning-making machinery of our psyches and our sub-cultures. He sees and shows, again and again, the unfulfilled promise that is in fact unfulfillable because it is a fantasy built upon a fantasy within a fantasy. It is not only the famous American formula of "life, liberty, and the pursuit of happiness" (which often gets reduced to such consumption-oriented caricatures as the dream of "home ownership" or "owning your own business"), but the human promise, the question of what a human life might mean, especially given the incessant and accelerating "progress" that none of us can escape. But, unlike the extravagant yet empty guarantees of every religion we personally do not believe in, the beguiling messages of advertising and marketing make more immediate, therefore more irresistible promises in the here and now, on this fully-sponsored planet Earth. As near as they seem to be to our grasp, Rodgers' work implies, the benefits extended by new technologies never profoundly touch us, except in our evanescent, anticipatory fantasies.

In the third world, where there are a few billion unique human beings for whom even a minimal level of what most Americans think of as "hope" is an unheard of, un-thought of luxury, the complex intellectual and spiritual frauds we know so well are not fully operative, but only present

11

in an innocent, embryonic, almost pure form. By contrast, in the world of Rodgers' paintings, a world dominated by the manufactured meaning that leisure allows for, the most interesting (because most self-aware) characters can actually be seen as having the equivalent of "no hope." They are caught in the fleeting, soon-forgotten moment of seeing that even the grandest, most motivating big ideas—love, happiness, and success—are cunningly designed, manufactured, packaged, distributed, and consumed. The notion of romance continues to be a marketable construction just like fashion, though mostly less organized and less branded. "Self-actualization," just like "weight-control," is the basis for an enormous service industry, and neither guarantees success, not because that would be bad for business (though it would) but because, as Rodgers puts it, "No one has a clue."

By nature, and by definition, we are foolish because we continually pursue the very phantoms we invent. Rodgers creates scenes in which these invisible spirits seem to haunt the figures, as if the disconnectedness of the individuals is part of a greater connectedness that they cannot see and can barely sense. What they know for sure is the lack, the missing parts, and the desire to be completed, fulfilled, at peace. In fact, the proverbial "wise person" savors the concept of freedom from desire, and practices transcending desire, as certain sages, saddhus, and shamans supposedly succeed in doing. Oscar Wilde's Young Fisherman said, "My desire is but for a little thing…I would send my soul away from me," but many of us are now far too sophisticated to think about such a simple thing as the soul, and we cannot allow ourselves for one moment to believe that we have title to one we could wish to give away, except that, now and then, we do feel the temptation to sell it. "Religion" and "Property" have been dominant ideas for centuries, then along came nationalism, patriotism, democracy, and freedom. Now we have the twenty-first century variation, "The War on Terror," promoted relentlessly by interested parties as if there is a reliable day-to-day significance for a person living their own unique and limited life. But Rodgers' work looks at local lives, privileged ones, certainly, but lives enmeshed in what Jean Baudrillard, in the Glaser translation, brilliantly calls "the invisible violence of security" (*Simulacra and Simulation* 57). Rodgers' paintings capture human experience at living instants, present psychological reality stripped of all generalities, and saturated in a lavish particularity that serves to underscore the futility of trying to have everything, trying to figure everything out, trying to learn how to manage one's unmanageable life.

We have arrived in the new century, and, even more grandiosely, "The New Millenium," having simply made more rapid but inevitable progress in a dull, unimaginative fashion by continuing to develop additional, ever-more-technically-precise concepts and practices. Rodgers argues that these ideas and capacities are no less romantic, fantastic, and fictive than any human constructs of the past. They are, as he puts it, "banal." In his view, we are still the same animals, behaving remarkably, behaving predictably, doing amazing tricks, doing what we've always done, and somehow sheltering and feeding and propagating ourselves, while operating ever more mystic machines. Rodgers points to examples of purist manias like those of male fundamentalists who protect their women by caging them in veils or invisible behavioral prisons, while calling up a competing construct on their laptops to help them forget what boredom they've created; Internet porn is the antidote to a brutally mandated, elaborately simulated (and utterly false) purity. Furthermore, there is the pervasive siren song of ultra-stylized adolescent pop music, a vague but all-encompassing medium that colors or even controls adolescent growth and development in recycled ideas and ever more insistent and superficially rebellious rhythms and lyrics, while reducing hip adults to continually re-learning a second language of culture.

Rodgers, despite the obvious disconnection among people that he so dramatically presents, is operating in a realm of universal connectivity. He sees a complex web of underlying forces that makes everything relate; he paints a multi-layered reality of which the human figures, because they are distracted by the splendid details of their existence, tend to be in ignorance. Rodgers believes that the contemporary *donnees* are no less grand, fantastic, and far-fetched than traditional romance and religion, but that they are based on more technical accomplishments and mechanisms, and delivered by more pervasive (or, more accurately, completely inescapable) media. The newest status quos of attitude and receptivity are merely backing support for an ensemble performance choreographed by an unimaginably successful commercial culture, in which the commodification of everything has been achieved, even personal principles. "Character" has become an accouterment that can be acquired via judicious seminar-shopping. In this sense, Rodgers is painting the metaphysical icons of an exploding culture, developing new conventions of representation that take on a meaning of their own. Sometimes, when we first view a Rodgers painting, all we see are unbelievable bodies and clothes and objects; but eventually we can believe Rodgers' paintings, once we begin to feel them, to apprehend the forces he's built in under the surfaces, as it were. Once felt, a Rodgers painting will often shadow us in every step of every day, in every passing thought, and every fragment of media intrusion. He teaches us a way of seeing, sifting, and interpreting the waves of stimulation we absorb.

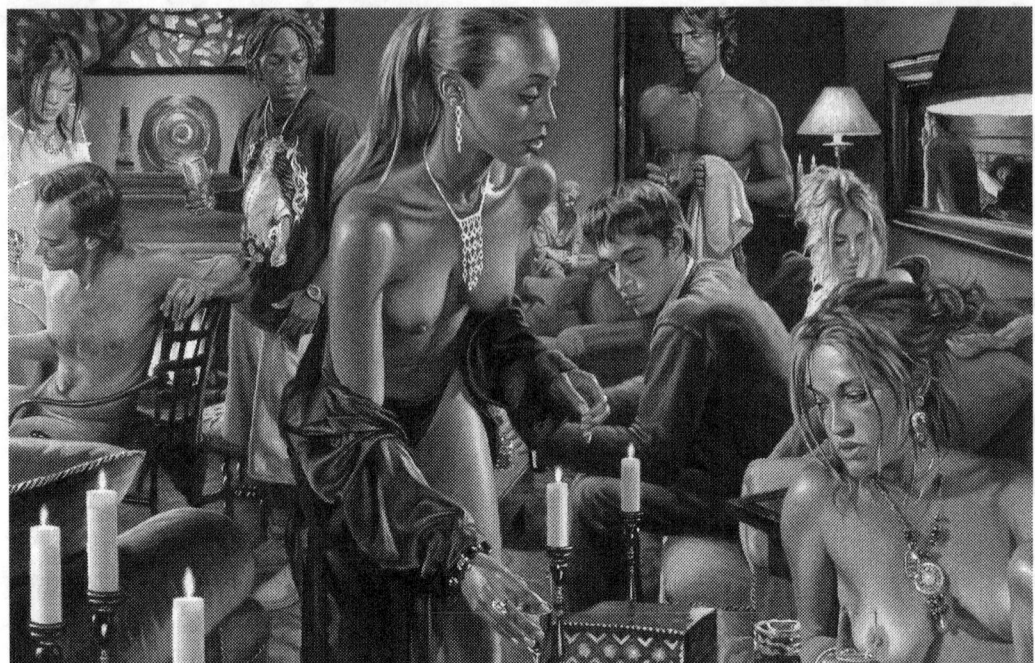

Fig. 2. *This Is Our Youth* (2004, 56" x 90")

Our Youth

Coming upon any large Rodgers canvas for the first time, a viewer unaccustomed to paintings with a dozen life-size figures (some of them only semi-clad), and in a setting that might be oddly archaic or over-the-top contemporary, is likely to be puzzled, if not exasperated, and *This Is Our Youth*, a canvas shown in Bologna in early 2004, is even more disorienting than most. Is this scene "real" or invented? Either way, how can we make sense of it? In *This Is Our Youth*, the viewer is confronted with eight compelling figures, including a naked man, three bare-chested figures, and a scantily-clad woman, all of them embodying a suggestion of "the beautiful." The aesthetically high-toned setting is apparently a room in a well-appointed contemporary house, full of art and artifacts and furniture—a room with red walls and red carpet. Where would the viewer possibly find such a scene?

What we may fail to ask is, "How do we typically make sense of our own complicated world?" How, in other words, do we interpret and react to our own local conditions? Only persons with rigid and unbending ideals of faith, order, or morality can possibly make the world conform to any model of their own comprehension, and that, by definition, involves quite a gigantic leap of faith.

The "party" metaphor is for Rodgers a way of representing the mind-bending, incomprehensible world we live in. Whether we consider social groups in trailer parks or palaces, the complexities are beyond our capacity to make sense of, just like these inexplicable party scenes.

The idea that these are either parties or fictions, however, is, from an art historical perspective, beside the point. They are ensembles, gatherings, settings, and poses that fit very well into the mainstream of art history; they are groups of people put together in one way or another by the painter's desire to make pictures, and "to get at something," as Rodgers puts it. His enthusiasm and awareness of the entire sweep of the history and scope of art activity excludes nothing, and embraces everything, including secular experimentation and religious orthodoxy.

Although *This Is Our Youth* accentuates the young, Rodgers is first and foremost a painter of the human. His paintings consistently deliver stunning figures, faces, and hands, as well as the hundred hues of human skin. He renders remarkable effects of both natural and artificial light, nimbly scattering shadow and brightness, and he combines colors with dazzling results, sometimes exploring a limited tonal range to suggest a mood. He creates magnificent effects with "drapery," the ways that fabric, hair, and jewelry are shaped by the force of gravity and against the human form. Above all, he achieves an irresistibly rendered painted surface, with juicy brushstrokes in one portion of a canvas and thinly-painted sections where the underpainting is visible, to conscious and canny effect.

Rodgers' sense of humor shows through, too. In the idiosyncratic object, the odd off-tone, the freaky trick of light, or the anomalous shadow, he will preserve what he finds in his observation and his photography, flouting what more careful or "tasteful" painters might consider better judgment. In *This Is Our Youth*, he presents a woman's nipple through a champagne glass, and the result is a double exposure, as he captures the refracted light through the glass. In his representations of human details, he preserves little aberrations in eyebrows, fingers, and knees, maintaining what he calls "veracity to the ways in which we're different." Even though, at first blush, these often-exposed people seem to be only "beautiful people," a closer inspection reveals the sometimes amusing, sometimes grotesque imperfections that make us endearing to our loved ones.

Each painting is a self-contained world that also functions as a cross-section of something indescribably immense, some kind of cosmic web, and it gives a weightiness to what at first glance can appear to be very light compositions. In the details of the paintings, there are material depths, and in the subtle juxtapositions and overall pictorial arrangements there is a spiritual and psychological breadth. The spectrum of skin tones is a world in itself, but the dynamics of the paintings and the feeling of movement and connection on a large scale create a sense of a larger, if multi-layered and even multi-dimensional unity. The figures and objects, including the plenitude of designer details, represent the wider world in ways that one recognizes days later—through a particular slant of light, spot of color, or curious (one is tempted to say "artificial") gesture. Everything is shattered (like the Julian Schnabel painting in the background), gathered, reflected (the carpet in the shiny metal of the table), refracted (the nipple in the glass), and included. It is a celebration of light: angles, sources, and reflections. *This Is Our Youth* and many other Rodgers paintings (e.g., *Shades of Olympus* and *American Rhapsody*) are like views inside a goldfish bowl that is densely packed with exotic creatures living their mysterious lives for us to watch.

The artwork quoted in *This Is Our Youth* functions both stylistically and symbolically. The sculpture in the center of the painting exudes interiority; it's more peaceful than the other figures, more present to its own sadness. It's both the effective experience of art and its cultural use as simple decoration, the same kind of decoration as the clothes and hair and jewelry, which, cumulatively and as a composite of something, are the only neutral aspect of the painting. Rodgers' painting is centered on all of this decorative accessorizing and thereby organized through it. The Nan Golden photograph on the right side of the painting serves as both a key and an echo. "That photo is no more real than the painting it's in," Rodgers remarks. The implication of the photograph is that the man and woman were recently intimate. And yet there is a sense of alienation between them. His back is to her. Their relation mirrors the sense we have of the figures in the room being internally focused. It's about the possibilities, or their lack, of relating to another human being, even in the most intimate of situations. In fact, people in a gallery viewing the Rodgers painting are in the same relation to it as the painted figures are to the photograph. The photo, with its fiery or heated color, is all the more ironic in relation to the cold state of the couple's unrelatedness. It's hot and cold at the same time. The Schnabel painting in the left corner is emblematic of decorative acquisitiveness, of status, and, in this painting, it forcefully represents a fractured world. We are borne back and forth within the painting between the Schnabel painting and the Golden photograph—carried in opposite directions by the conceptual dynamics Rodgers has built into the work.

This Is Our Youth is about the difficulty of connection, certainly, but it is also about its possibility. Each character seems tied by their attention to someone else in the room. The vectors of their glances and gestures and postures generate an intense energy amidst apparent languor. But whatever connectivity there is, it's clearly fragile, so tenuous that it might be only the remains of a shattered intimacy. That ghost of connection or relation is both hot and cold, successful or not, positive or negative, encouraged by love or driven by resentment, even hatred. This painting is about the tenuous aspects of relating and connecting, and, by casting the human crew in the category of "youth," Rodgers highlights notions of innocence and experience, as American culture itself is both young and jaded.

Shades of Olympus and Second Sight

Among the paintings shown in Amsterdam in the fall of 2004 were two arresting large canvases that epitomize Rodgers' most recent work and embody many of his interests over the past fifteen years. Both have a lot to say about the America of the new millennium. "I love to mess with the culture," Rodgers admits. He is particularly interested in "the myth of perfectibility" and "the infinitude of choices" that characterize the current American scene. In *Shades of Olympus*, Rodgers employs the image of Paris Hilton on the left side of the canvas as a kind of false anchor for the complicated composition, which, despite its intricacy, exudes a peaceful feeling. On the right, the scene is a vortex of forces and details, and there is no apparent sign of serenity or order, especially because of the full frontal male nudity backlit by the elegant fireplace. But on the left, Rodgers presents an apparently ordered world that is obviously a construct with little connection to human experience. It is as if Paris Hilton is a cartoon version of American culture, an icon and a caricature all at once. But on the right, in the intricacies and complexities of the figures, objects, and intra-pictorial spaces, Rodgers explores what he calls "the magic of paint in relation to reality." By this he means the many "criss-cross effects" that are created both by brushstrokes and spatial arrangement. Even though the glances are disconnected—no one makes eye contact in a Rodgers painting—there is an implied connection in the overlapping bodies and the rhythmic gentleness of the light rippling across the Asian woman's vulnerable chest. The sum total of the many unconnected glances is an interlocking web of intricate, intimate, and inevitable human connection. The end result is a delicacy of crazy visual rhythms that can have a vaguely soothing effect in a certain section of the canvas, even while generating a disturbance somewhere else.

Similarly, *Second Sight* conveys an immediate sense of clashing parts, a maelstrom of emotion, and a suspicion of imperceptible realities, while ultimately suggesting the possibility of some kind of transcendental insight or inarticulate understanding. The figures seem isolated but not lonely; they seem engaged in something, even if it's not interaction with one another. These people are in a place where the competition is potentially vicious and their shelf life (as desirable, consumable personages) possibly brief. There is a hint of suspicion in the eyes of the man on the upper right. Perhaps, beyond the frame of the canvas, something is happening that slightly threatens him. The legs of the central female figure create disorder in the center of the canvas, and they clash with the light belly of the woman behind (not to mention the confusion of the wineglass, the hand, and her pelvis) to further dislocate the arrangement. Other arms, as if all akimbo, exaggerate the clashing effect. The eyes of the woman in the right foreground could be looking at the viewer or just past, creating that awkward moment when we wonder if we should respond to a stranger's glance, or if it isn't us she's looking at after all. Something might or might not be about to begin, and the curtain in the background suggests the same possibility, of a magic show that might be ready to take place. But the look in the eyes of the tall blonde as she seems to regard the seated man on the phone suggests the possibility of resentment, or at least of disappointment—that something isn't quite going her way.

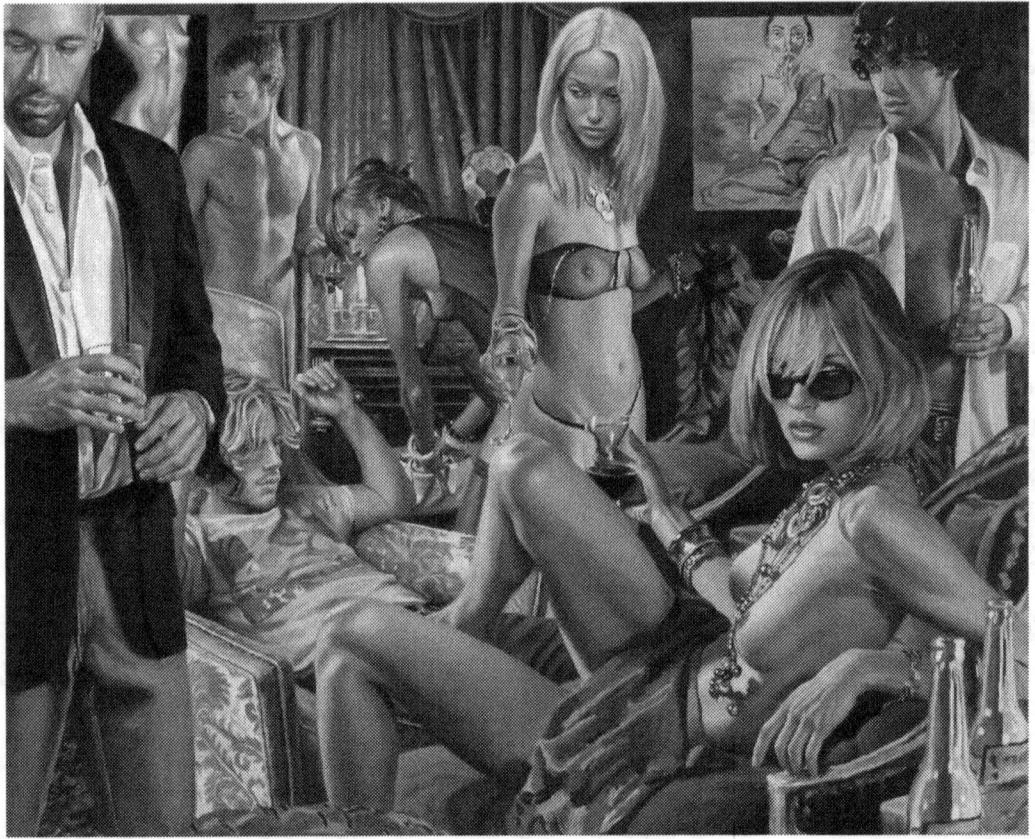

Fig. 3. *Second Sight* (2004, 63" x 80")

Second Sight is a microcosm of a competitive culture that is characterized by tension and sometimes blindness. It would require some kind of extra-sensory perception to figure out what is going on here, and the way we live now affords precious little opportunity for any kind of first sight, given the numerous preoccupations and demands.

"Nobody is simply self-reflective," Rodgers says. "Perhaps they've given up. The explanations of what goes on around us are inevitably inadequate," he adds. "We're all faced with the inexplicable." Rodgers is drawn to moments and personalities in which, more often than not, there is a lack, but it isn't a specific, known lack that could be remedied. And, in the case of the rare individual whose wants are carefully formulated, this world isn't likely to satisfy those wants. "People's internal needs are thwarted more often than not," Rodgers observes. "We think we are supposed to be able to get what we want, but no matter how many seminars we attend, we can't quite figure it out." Rodgers paints people who are competing, who are programmed to try and try and try, but who are also committed to looking cool, as if they aren't trying, as if they have nothing to lose.

The interior party pictures are a special world unto themselves, from which the viewer is always apparently excluded, then drawn in, and eventually entranced by. The fact that we are confronted with life-size and larger figures has a powerful effect, both pushing us farther away physically and pulling us in psychologically. It is difficult to remain "at a distance" from such substantial human figures; their size encourages us to relate to them. To some extent, a lighthearted, self-conscious, voyeuristic attitude is what Rodgers' works encourage us to adopt, and, as it turns out, this posture will allow us to more fully penetrate these ensembles. However, only a dedication to seeing and re-seeing will allow us truly to be admitted, person by person, and brushstroke by brushstroke. The overall effect is the painter's vision of things as they are and as they will be, like an X-ray of the surface of life that reveals the combining forces of pure, direct experience under the influence of a thousand, mostly unnoticed variables. The details Rodgers revels in—what Rilke referred to as the "smallest constituent element" or "the cell"—honor the history of painting and show the way in. The macrocosm may seem impenetrable, but through the details we can gain entrance and find our way around at a microcosmic level.

In a sense, Rodgers is re-modernizing painting via a combination of the high-culture figurative tradition and the occasional nods to pop art that signal his disdain for the stuffiness and elitism of merely theoretical abstraction and conceptual dead ends. His work, like pop art, democratizes the process by inviting everyone in to look. His use of contemporary and traditional art references in the paintings provides markers and a respectful, even enthusiastic tribute to art of all kinds. As the age of terror has intensified, Rodgers' groupings have become more dense, and the individuals more exposed. His density of ensemble is reminiscent of certain classical painters and old masters, like Michelangelo, Raphael, Botticelli, and Rembrandt, who developed or inherited conventions of organization. Narrative, history, and genre painting all offer precedents for what he does; even Hogarth's "The Rake's Progress" comes to mind. Rodgers' pictorial organization is becoming a genre unto itself, as he continues to experiment with density, arrangement, and depth. When asked about a painting of his, Rodgers will frequently begin, in a tone not of bravado but sincere delight, "This is a perfect painting." By this, the artist, who lacks nothing in confidence but is also profoundly modest, seems to mean that he has, first, arrived at a conceptual vision that pleases him, and second, painted it to his satisfaction.

One of the galleries that has recently recognized Rodgers' remarkable accomplishments and exceptional promise is Milan's Marella Arte Contemporanea. Their Fall 2003 show, "Vectors of Desire," was a sensational success, and it suggested the usefulness of a study like the present one. As Maria Rosa Marella put it, "We fell in love with Terry's work at The Armory Show in New York. He's a strong and intriguing painter." Primo Marella went on to say, "We were delighted to bring him to Italy, and the reaction here was, as we expected, tremendously enthusiastic. He presents fascinating people in interesting situations, and the way he handles paint is superb." Marella plans to mount another Rodgers show in 2005.

Crowded as they are in the large, dense pictures, the Rodgers characters' only opportunity to exert control in their limited world is by means of posture, gesture, and facial expression: small moves, careful moves, calculated moves. An attitude of appearing to fit in, the ethos of an ensemble performance, essentially. Gallery-goers, collectors, and interviewers often want to know about the nature and origin of these gatherings Rodgers paints. In fact, these groups of people are both as real and as fantastic as those in *The Bathers*, *Dejeuner sur l'herbe*, *The Joy of Life*, and *The Boat Party*. They are as real as *Guernica*. They are realistic fictions, fabrications, fantasies. They are symbolic representations of reality just like ordinary speech is, just like a poem or song lyric or advertisement. Just like life.

2. The Culture of Desire

---

*"I love to look at us looking, and I'm fascinated by what
we think we see, and what we think is missing."*
—Terry Rodgers

Rodgers is interested in the way humans covet and crave, and in the objects of their desire; and he is interested in the origins and forces of desire, in everything from suppressed sexual passion to the "hunger" for a new pair of shoes. Even more compelling for the artist, however, is the fact that he views desire as the medium of human experience, despite loud and well-formulated denials by individuals and organizations alike, thereby creating a web of confusion in which human beings are caught. This ever-present, collective perplexity is characterized by the absolute impossibility of human judgment, given the elaborate quality of the images, constructs, fantasies, and outright fictions—and the staggering quantities of the sources of stimulation. The stimuli include anything anyone yearns for or sees value in, anything desirable, worth having or seeking, anything arousing desire, including but not limited to the usual assumption that most desire has a sexual origin.

What do the Rodgerian figures wish for, hope for, incline toward, or need? What inspires their interests, enthusiasms, passions—their dreams, fantasies, imaginations? What tempts them? What makes them euphoric or ecstatic? Defeated, desperate? What makes their hearts race, skip a beat, or sink? What do they love? Rodgers investigates all of this in all of its infinite complexity with a relentless energy and a creative, completely non-reductive curiosity unmatched by any other living painter, and he does it without any pretense of supplying the correct answer.

Everything and Everyone

Rodgers understands the larger world as a place of infinite connectivity, and he sees the details of the smallest setting as mirroring that large-scale web. On the one hand, he brings us into a fuller awareness of the way we are related; on the other, one never finds two Rodgers figures looking at one another, much less touching. A brief survey of a few recent paintings can indicate how he succeeds in embodying the whole world in his paintings of highly local, frequently interior, and apparently exceptional situations.

All About Eve is a painting in which the four men and the dominant female figure will not meet our eyes. They look down, avoiding us, and avoiding each other. In fact, this downward-turned glance is common to most Rodgers paintings. (A rare exception to this dominant tendency is in *A Question of Style*; this painting, which includes a Rodgers self-portrait, features a young woman looking powerfully into our eyes with a directness made all the more forceful and penetrating by its rarity in Rodgers' work.) Observers of Rodgers' work often remark on the disconnectedness of the figures. And yet his figures betray none of the radical discontinuities of Matisse's *Le Bonheur de Vivre* (*The Joy of Life*), of which Jack Flam wrote, "…the various figures are curiously disconnected; and many seem quite unaware of each other's existence" (*Great French Paintings from the Barnes Foundation* 226). What Rodgers sees is what he calls a "connected disconnectedness" that humans have always struggled against, but one that has somehow become more intense and more poignant for all of the means of communication now available to us. And it is this elusive connectivity that we have in common, which amplifies (and makes more poignant) the fact of our inability to identify what is important, or to reliably compare notes on it.

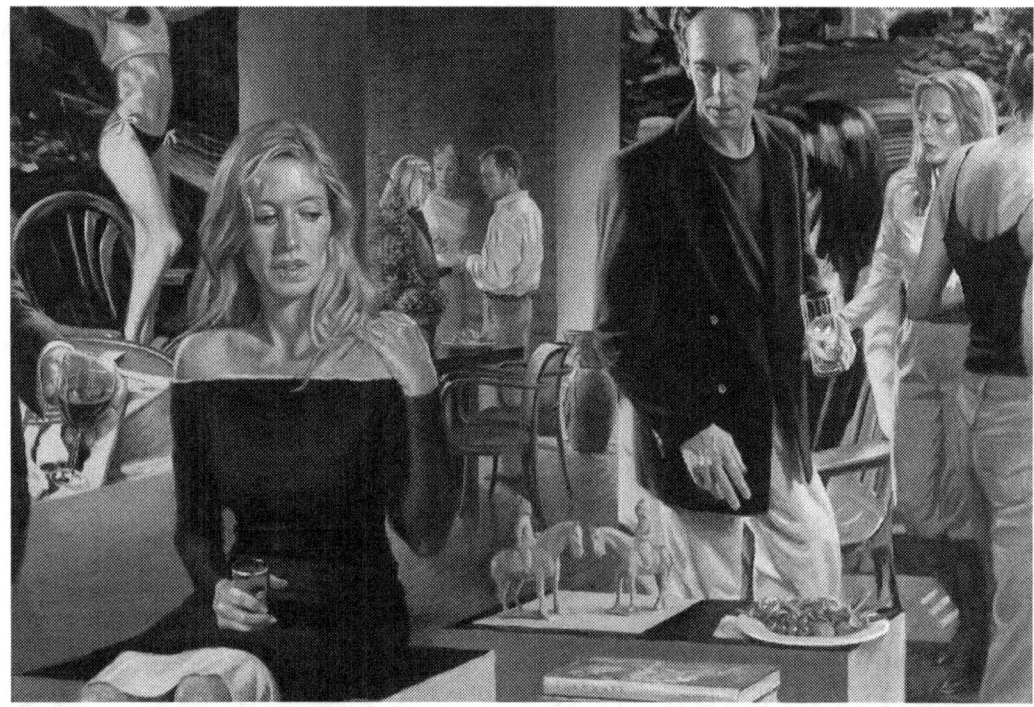

Fig. 4. *The Definite Article* (2001, 52" x 79")

The idea of "the real thing," as Henry James put it, or *The Definite Article*, as Rodgers' painting has it, suggests that we encounter people who may, according to someone's lights, be the definite article or the real thing, or they may simply be really trying very hard to seem to be the real thing—we can't tell. Perhaps they feel as if they are the real thing, and that if they could just find someone else who is as real as they are, everything would be all right. "The" is the definite article, of course, and it suggests that you're going to follow it with a definition, but this situation is indefinite. We can't know who they are and what's going on. Maybe they can't know themselves. The worst of it is, even if we knew both of the central figures, we would keep thinking we know the story when in fact there is probably more going on. There is a rhythm of horses and their riders head-to-head, echoing the two figures in black. The suggestion is a little bit like a cartoon's balloon thought. Various people and objects are putting thoughts into other people's heads— reading minds, misreading minds—and there is this rhythm (1-2, 1-2, 1-2…), the great divide, and everything's in motion, and everything's in stasis, caught like photos and sculpture. At the bottom of human experience is the desire to have one's own experience validated by someone we trust: someone else, because we can't trust ourselves. We need what we will never achieve: a full-scale revolution of unprecedented proportions to change the way we think, the way we interact, the way we make bad deals, and the way in which we agree to disagree and then blame it on each other, as if we were somehow exceptional in our failure.

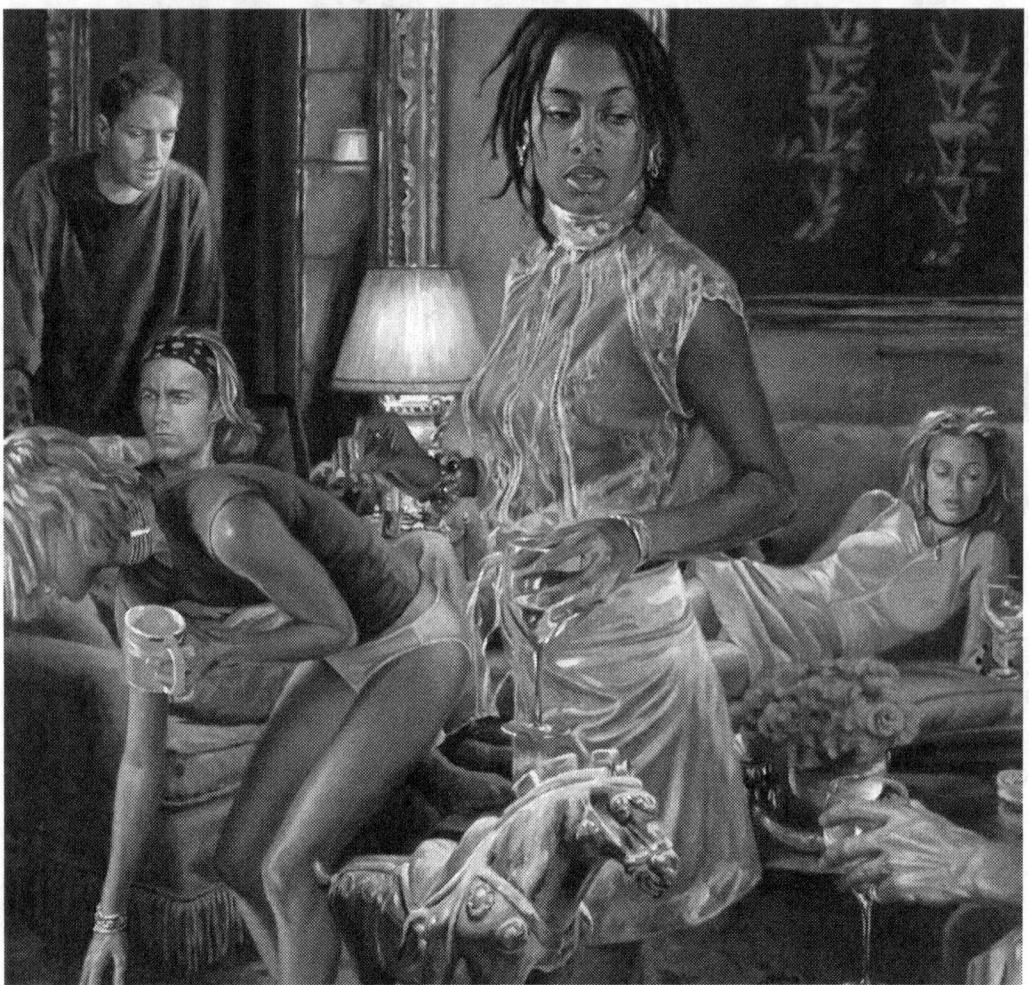

Fig. 5. *Cartesian Coordinates* (2003, 61 ½" x 66")

Failing a completely revolutionary transformation that will once and for all right everything that is wrong with us, we can evolve via the comparatively serene approach of *Cartesian Coordinates*, which offers us a grid to locate ourselves and secure our bearings, to finally find ourselves. The X and Y axes are constituted by an older culture, or even several prior cultures. The past, from the vantage of the present, was more orderly. The past can place these figures in a world, a grid, a context, as suggested by the various horizontals and verticals of the background. This suggests their being caught and measured. The girl on the couch is the antithesis of the old world. Her breasts defy the old order and the X and Y constraints. Their liquid flow represents the contradiction by a youthful reality of a constrained, invented, orderly universe. The disorder of youth, of the body, and of humanity in general is so different from the cultivated rigidities, from the old, implacable desire for order. The one component of the picture that shows up in the violations of the youth culture and both connects to and mirrors the clear definitions of the older culture is the completely vertical, magnificent central figure. She represents the clarity of being with her uprightness and her firm, clear look. She's not a servant or a slave to what's going on in this scene. She is regal, noble, transcendent. The connection between the youthful disorder and the old order in this black female figure is focused in her eyes. She ties it together in some ineffable way (some crux or paradox). It's about seeing clearly, and that's what she stands for: the black woman is paradoxically representing both underclass and aristocracy. Rodgers observes, "At its worst, this is a painting of puns." At its best, it captures the grids of the present, fixing each of us in the axes that we measure ourselves by, and showing us again and again that we don't measure up. The only thing we can do to save ourselves is to cease our incessant, unsettling calculations. Think, but observe the thoughts we have, and don't desire too much from them or they will exasperate, aggravate, and disappoint us.

But even the desire to be free from desire is in itself a disturbing desire, and, in that sense, desire is a key component that is inherent in the human condition, perhaps even "natural." More insidious than any natural desire are the "unnatural" or man-made desires, the pre-fabricated ones, the ones that are nevertheless deeply-rooted, so that they are in effect a fundamental part of the culture we are born into. These, because they serve someone's purpose, are relentlessly enforced through social conditioning. Rodgers discovered this as an adolescent, having grown up in a suburban American culture that succeeded in masking much of the spectrum of human experience. But his own personal inclinations and circumstances led to him lifting the mask, poking around behind the façade, and generally discovering the way things did not seem but were. Born in 1947, Rodgers saw the Fifties turn to the Sixties from the edge of Washington, D.C., where the America we know today was under energetic construction.

"Growing up in the burgeoning suburbs of Washington gave me a front row seat at the roaring edge of the game," Rodgers wrote to me recently. "From the roads and woods disappearing to the metastasizing developments, out of farmers' fields and having no history, or even old buildings, upon which to build any orientation, it was the fiction of the Fifties moving always towards the bigger and the newest. There was no old town out in Maryland. It was westward expansion into a void. I saw the houses being made, but few others did. Most people I knew never understood how anything was made or accomplished. No one even knew what their dad did. It's the same old story now, the vagueness of growing up in the suburbs. We don't know anything except all of the appropriate behaviors for fitting in with whatever our surroundings are, and I happened to see this just when my consciousness started setting in, and then I began to notice everyone dealing (or not dealing) with it. And then I realized that people dealt with it (or lived with it rather than dealt with it) forever."

Rodgers' increasing interest in observation and making things led to an interest in art that took him out of the suburbs. "I went to the Corcoran on Saturdays during my high school years and discovered more about this looking/painting thing that had a grip on me. The most amazing time was drawing a large black woman, nude, in class. She had a full, rippling stomach, curving around her, with absolutely wonderful, undulating shapes, exactly what the growing world of the suburbs seemed designed to disallow one from seeing or experiencing. It was like the real versus the semi-real, the earth versus pure plasticity, or sense versus senselessness, or something like that."

The frantic destruction of wilderness and cultivation of civilization in America frames the competition between the spiritual and the material in Rodgers' work. Either the first or last resort of desire is the purely spiritual and even self-sacrificing. The native American, John Wannuaucon Quinney, in his Independence Day Speech of 1854, expressed the ultimate desire: "to die in hope." This was a man taking American citizenship near the end of his life so that he could have title to a small parcel of land that the Mohicans had always called home. No longer was his desire to have the intruders leave, or to have his old way of life back; he simply desired to die "in hope." John Dewey noted a two-step process in the formation of such a recognizable desire: "Obstruction of the immediate execution of the impulse converts it into a desire." Impulse and desire—neither are anything like the planned purpose with which the suburbs get built on old Indian ground. Capitalism, with all of its detailed intention, is all about delayed gratification and intermittent reinforcement. Rodgers sees the civilized interior lives of suburban Americans and paints faces and figures and objects as if they were rocks, trees, and clouds. Instead of the landscape, Rodgers gives us the humanscape, and his brushstrokes evoke the elements, the forces of wind and rain and sun. All of it is about human desire in ever-changing, ever more artificial surroundings.

If desire is the climate we live in, how do we understand it? Recognizing our desires is a problem of cognition. We need help. We have therapists, videotape, and Rodgers' paintings. But, even given insight, can we exert control on desire? Can we understand the forces well enough to control them? Is the power of desire essentially internal and propulsive, or is it external and attractive, powered by some as-yet-undiscovered magnetic force; do we drive toward the objects of our desire, or are we drawn in by them? Or are we essentially funneled in the directions we eventually travel by forces conspiring and combining to send us along in some complicated, compromised, consolidated way? Or, perhaps the favorite possibility these days, is it something far beyond chronological, cultural, and interpersonal forces? Are we simply programmed by our genetic content, or the collective-unconscious, or misremembered *deja vus*?

To explore questions like these, Rodgers likes to highlight what he calls the "inner-outer dichotomy": "We're always assuming we can tell what's going on inside another person based on their exterior appearance. We judge a book by its cover—that's one of the great human activities. We think we have nothing else to go on. And so it's like the hell of being human is always misinterpretation, even misinterpretation of our own motives, situations, and moods." Regarding the Freudian notion of "displaced" or "dislocated" desires, Rodgers prefers to expand the concept beyond the merely erotic and sexual: "We have the natural proclivity to make surface interpretations, and, at the same time, we have been commercially conditioned to see 'the inside' in terms of acquisitions, physical attributes, style, and surface. And what that means is that we automatically judge by looking, and 'the commercial enterprise' has latched on to that and used it so that designers can consciously or unconsciously employ it to attach meaning and value and fulfillment to very specific products, locations and sizes of homes, body types, skin color, motor vehicles, delectability of lips. And that's the entire inner-outer dichotomy on steroids."

"We naturally look at people and misjudge," he says, "and now our culture has taken that even further, and we are distracted and confused by it. It helps misdirect us. It inhibits fulfillment. It doesn't prevent it. It confuses us in our search for fulfillment." Rodgers sees social and sexual messages everywhere, the latter as if fulfilling Freud's prescription for a confused psyche. "Seduction has two sides," Rodgers observes, "the fundamental and human side of the person, which is attractive, and the specialized side, where style, perfection, and codes start to supplant a valid interaction. There are real people and then there is the ideal image of perfection—both legitimately seductive. To be real is desirable; to be perfect is desirable, if unrealistic. You get this experience of the individual that is somehow caught between these two warring sides."

Genuine experience is completely other than what Rodgers calls "codes of perfection" embedded in objects and images, all of which is legitimately seductive, but embodying a promise that will only disappoint. Attractiveness is legitimate, in Rodgers' view, because it's an unavoidable part of humanity, but the idea of it is often misused, and, he observes, "We're caught in the middle: attraction is the subject; seduction is the issue. Allure. Women's equipment. Tactility. It's all about the wish to touch and have and how we think we're entitled to perfection."

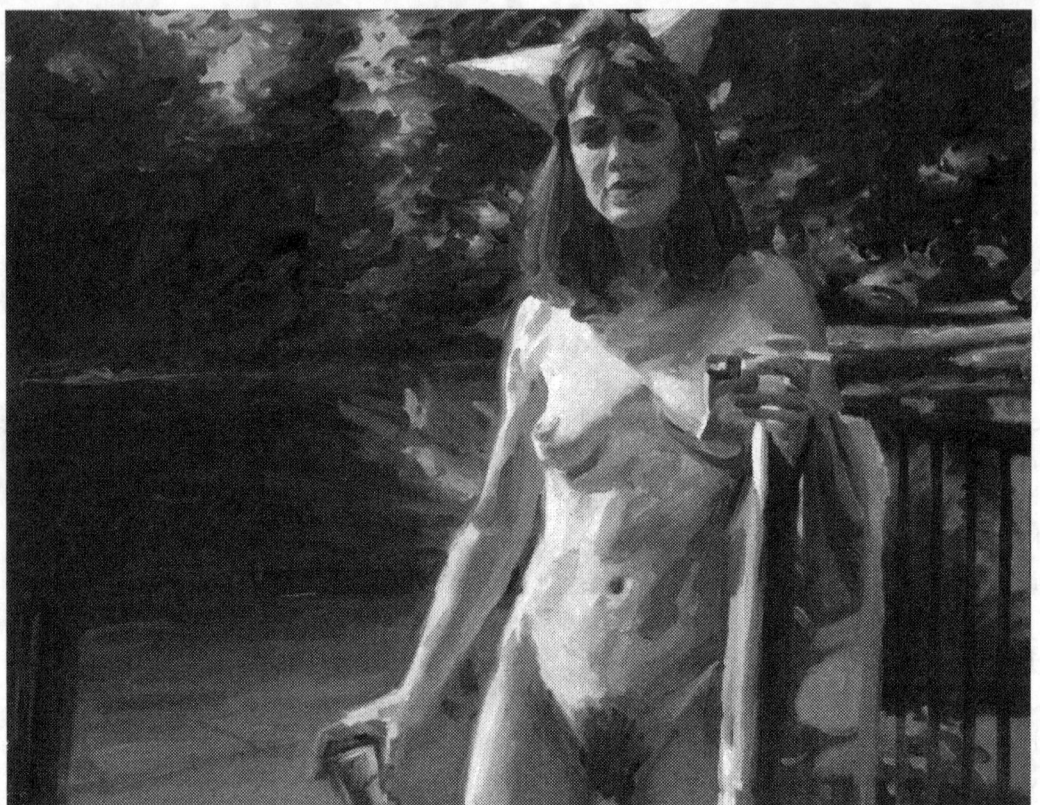

Fig. 6. *Elizabeth* (1991, 40" x 60")

As a prime example of this, Rodgers points to *Elizabeth*, the portrait of a strikingly individual and real person (and, incidentally, a naked woman) painted almost abstractly. The subject is not a typically "pretty" woman with the Armani stamp of approval. This painting, more than any of the others, is about the viscosity of the paint defining the subject's presence rather than any conventional ideas about beauty. In Rodgers' view, the application of the paint is one of the many languages through which we can actually perceive and appreciate an image, a person, or anything else, as they are rendered through paint. "The magic of ideals creates some prejudices and exaggerates others," Rodgers says. "Having the perfect skirt or genetically perfect face, or baring the right piece of flesh, does not necessarily produce the personal satisfaction that was promised. So there's this constant push-pull within which we live."

Some people would call this kind of full frontal nudity "confrontational," but *Elizabeth* has a much more intimate effect. The subject seems far more present than many of Rodgers' subjects. "You can see and sense the person beneath the cultural stuff, the accouterments, the schtick of the party hat and cigarettes," he says. The paint is both abstract and defining (pictorial), so that this picture is both an abstraction in the paint and a person in her being. The abstraction of the paintiness itself is like a slurpy, loose, moving, oleaginous extravaganza on the surface level. The technique entirely reinforces her naked comfort, with the result that she appears unusually present in her body and in her head.

Elizabeth highlights what Rodgers has recuperated of the meaning of realism in relation to the now-familiar meaning of abstraction. He has answered Baudrillard's accusation that we have lost these meaningful distinctions. "Something has disappeared," Baudrillard wrote, "the sovereign difference, between one and the other, that constituted the charm of abstraction." Rodgers has restored something of that charm by practicing a disciplined realism punctuated by illuminating doses of abstraction. Knowing the painter, one might even turn that observation on its head and say that he practices an abstraction that is punctuated by doses of what we call realism, of what we construe to be recognizable people and places. The subject of *Elizabeth* is abstractly presented, with the paradoxical effect that, given our all-too-real-world, always-in-focus, high-decibel culture, this woman is more human than anyone revealed to us through reality television.

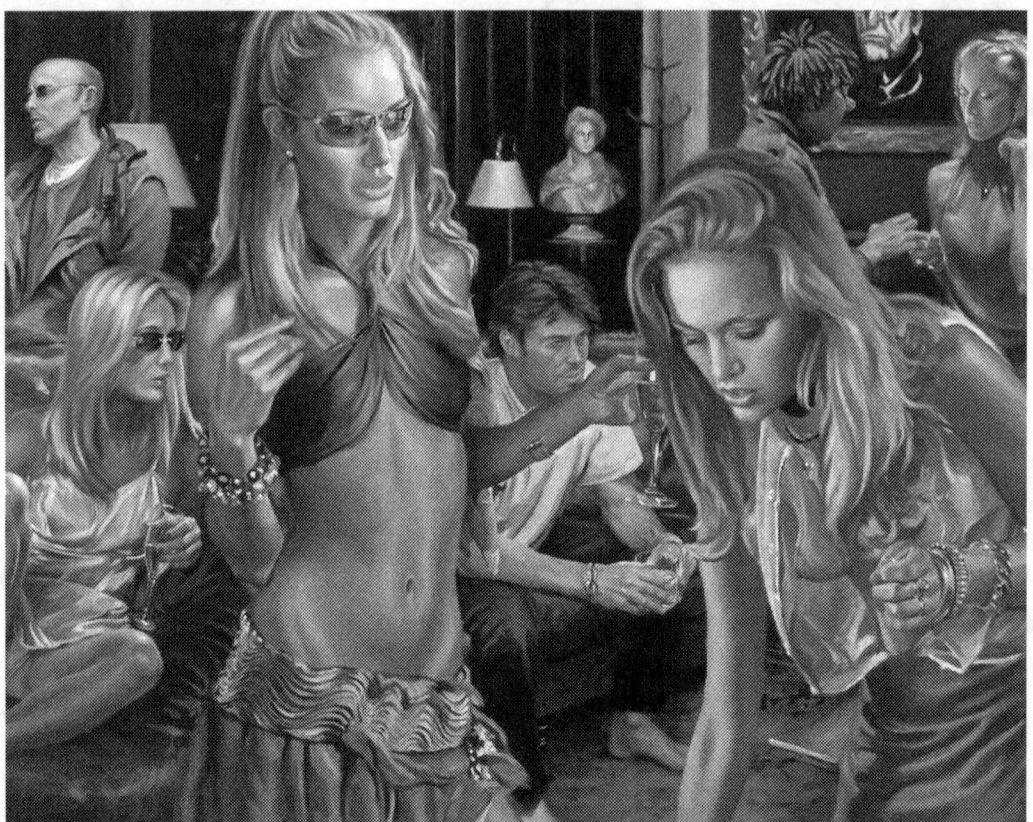

Fig. 7. *The Dialogues* (2003, 56" x 72 ½")

In the face of the uncertainty, incomprehension, disorientation, and what Rodgers calls "unknowability" of our daily lives, *The Dialogues* is one of Rodgers' most optimistic statements about the possibility of self-realization in this transparently and transcendently artificial age. Here, unlike most Rodgers' paintings, there is actual and intense dialogue. Even of those not obviously speaking, everybody seems somehow engaged and, again, contrary to many of Rodgers' scenes, not so much preoccupied as occupied, as if involved in the notion of how to collectively disport themselves for this occasion, the women in their sexy outfits, the men in their macho casual sloppy negligent wear: urban outdoors nonchalant. There is a high degree of attention paid here: to clothing, behavior, and display. The space is an older-style room, and the personal style is that of putting themselves forward, and in both cases the style is the backdrop for what their actual interests are. By their faces, it's clear that they're paying attention, especially the background figures. There are two looking across the room with a kind of TV urgency, as if something compelling is on. That would be unusual for Rodgers. There is never any TV. Or is someone talking in an animated fashion?

The semi-disclosed, half-hidden, wonderfully enveloped breast is spectacular, fascinating, mysterious, with shadows so deftly painted. It is hidden and revealed, like their lives. The intimacy of the partly exposed breast is an emblem of something sacred, personal, genuine. The sculpture is part of the interior look, suggesting an out-of-fashion desire from previous generations or centuries, clearly an antique, taking us back from the twenty-first century to a long-lost culture. The picture in the background is a Francis Bacon, much more contemporary and angst-ridden. The face lives there as a ghost, haunting the past, present, and future. It hovers with an ominous quality, like a shade, threat, memory, or presentiment of death. The background of life is death. Most of the background is death: night, dark, lost, past. Everything outside their interactive light moves off into something that is uncertain and unknowable. The breast, partially revealed, is the unknowable almost known.

It's fascinating to think of Rodgers in relation to Bacon. In 1962, when Bacon's work went against the grain, David Sylvester wrote, "It's not out of a desire to be chic that so many painters of the human image today play it cool, do it satirically. They know how nearly impossible it has become to paint solemn images of man's fate when newsreels and news photos are constantly bombarding us with pictures of tribulation and disaster hot from the hells of the world, making the calamitous image an inflationary currency—in much the same way as the ubiquity of the pin-up has made it embarrassing to paint a beautiful woman beautifully." To "paint a beautiful woman beautifully" might well be a motto of Rodgers, with the amendment that he often adds the slightest suspicion of physical irregularity or tonal anomaly, just to highlight and challenge the viewer's ideas of artificial feminine beauty. And Rodgers ignores all of the contemporary incarnations and variations on "newsreels." He disdains television. Twenty-four-hour cable TV is of no interest to him, and that allows him to paint without concern about Sylvester's "newsreels" running amok.

Sylvester, in the same piece, says of Bacon (but it might as well be about Rodgers), "But beyond the conscious will to make the thing particular, he has a knack for finding images that unite the vitality of a particular form with the resonance of a general import. Bacon, everyone feels (whether they like his work or not), is saying something that matters about the times in which we live—perhaps about the vulnerability that dangerously qualifies the arrogance of those in power. Yet nothing is more improbable than that he is setting out to moralise or enlighten. He is obviously an artist in whom compulsion is far stronger than intention, an artist ruled by private obsessions." Sylvester goes on to talk about "those ruling monsters we see as father-figures." For Rodgers, the "ruling monsters" are less a class of certain powerful people than they are certain powerful attitudes and concepts and vernaculars: fashion, form, appearance, conformism, and the obsession with a putative nonconformist commercial faith that results in a kind of cattle call.

The middle and foreground of *The Dialogues* is characterized by vitality, with focused people congregating in intense, living moments. Their brains and personalities are engaged, and yet what we're looking at—breast and stomach and thigh displaying themselves—has a background of death and a foreground mortality, wrapped in flesh that will decay. That stomach: an impenetrable wall of flesh. But the breast is the delicate side of a fragile, physical being, semi-covered and semi-protected, yet it shows up almost like the poignant interior of the person, looking at her body, intimately, and her soul, her heart, so much more vulnerable than the other woman, so delicate. It indicates the poignancy of being self-consciously human in this universe. It shows the heart of tenderness among what might easily be cool New York conversations that verge on the cold. That breast is the star of the show: the sequence of hand to breast to armpit is so interestingly arranged, and the breast itself is painted like a Cezanne fruit. There is an ultimate dialogue between every shape and object and texture and idea. The dialogues we don't have in words are the most important ones going on today. The connections we don't take the time to make are the most crucial to our well-being in a time of frantic connectivity.

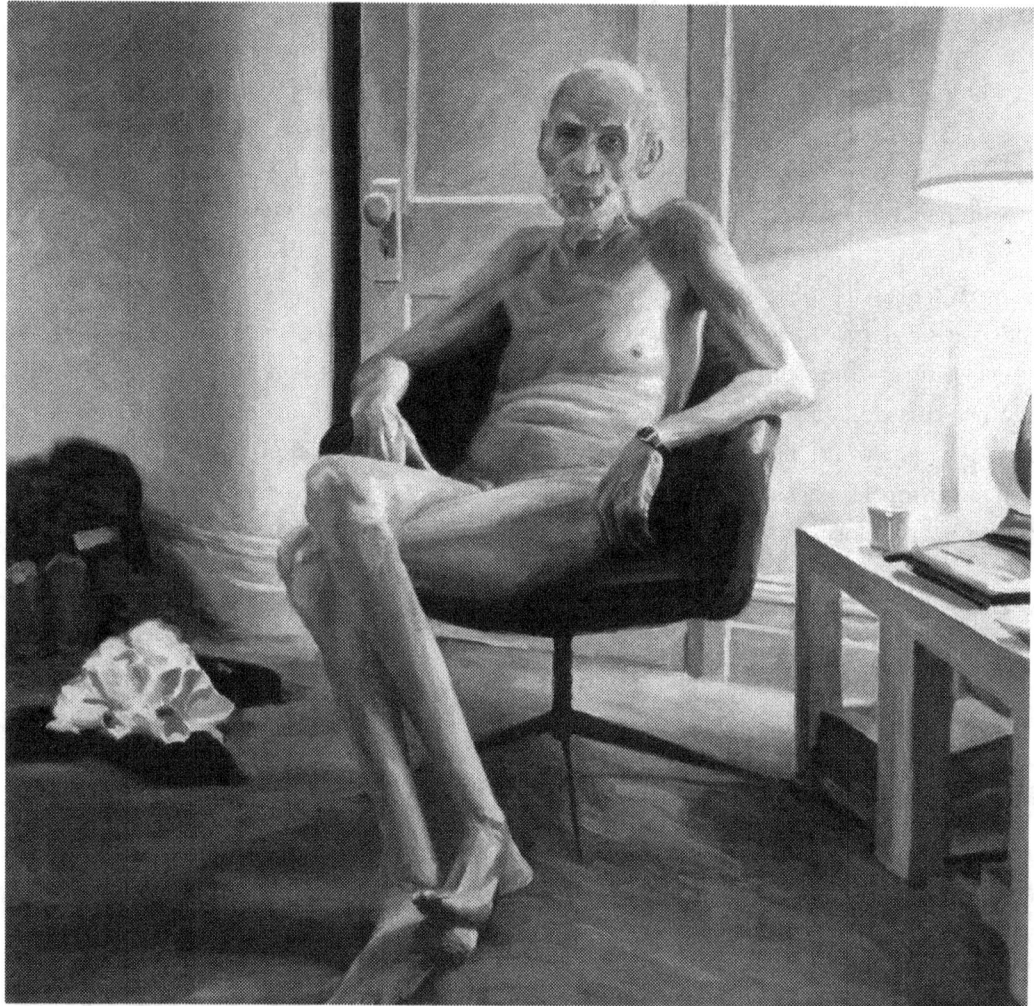

Fig. 8. *Timepiece* (1995, 68" x 72")

One of Rodgers' greatest achievements is a tribute to the human spirit in the face of mortality, or even fatality: *Timepiece*. Like *Elizabeth*, this single-figure painting shows an individual in isolation, but not isolated in a group. He is alone, by himself, dramatically removed from anyone who can either promise to help him, or disappoint him by not delivering what he thought they might. Here is a man as he has to face himself every day. "He's not nineteen and buff and turning people's heads," says Rodgers. "He's at a much later stage in life. He is that person that we all have to deal with in ourselves." Unlike a Diane Arbus subject, he wasn't born into this kind of grotesque body, but he has grown into it, and he is now no longer socially acceptable.

The old man of *Timepiece* represents the terminus of desire for everyone fortunate enough to get there, reminiscent of the native American Quinney's desire "to die in hope." (The subject was actually dying of cancer, and he died soon after the painting was completed.) This is about acceptance, realization. You have the facts—his fragility, his decrepitude—that he deals with. You have the searing light of revelation coming in from the right, blindingly. You can't avoid the poignant eyes in the center, and you can see these big relics of the strength that he had—the monolithic hand—relics from time past (and the watch accentuates that passing time!) with the contrasting frailness of his shoulders and his bony, toothpick legs, and then his feet and toes. And against this decaying figure is an almost mystical background, featuring the exit door with the black shadow to the left, the black chair he sits in, the black pile to the left, and three black spikes beneath him. His desires are all inward now, tied together in the ultimate reflective convergences of elegiac memory and looming, dooming mystery.

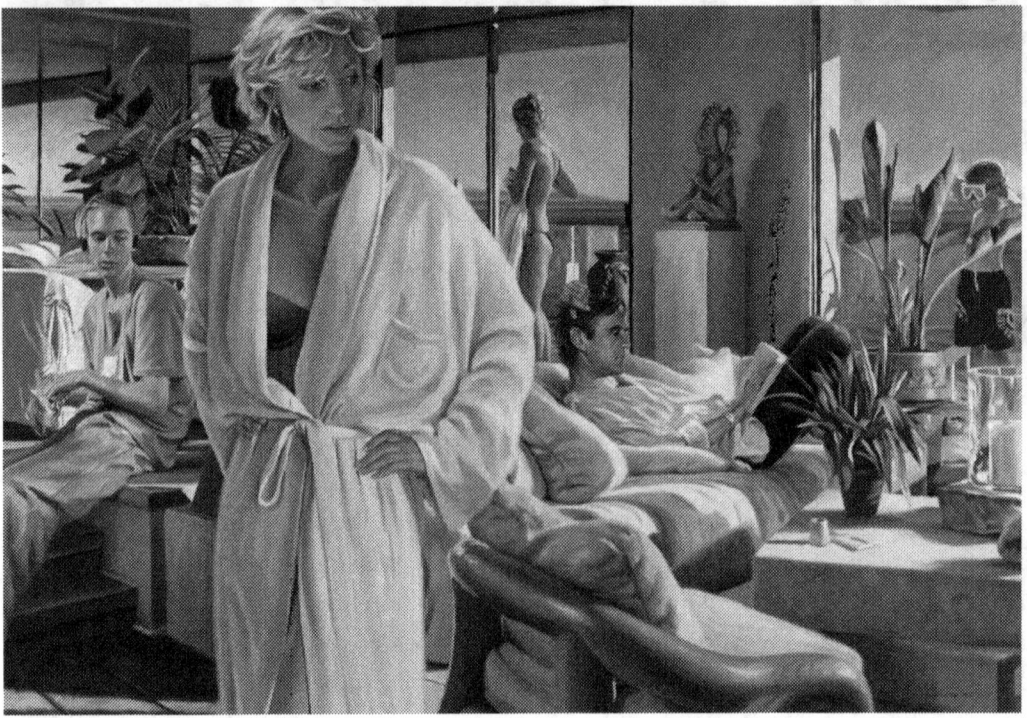

Fig. 9. *Sound of the Sea* (2002, 54" x 80 ½")

We have desires all day long, our whole life through. Call them wishes, wants, passions, inclinations, appetites, or needs. We might even have them in our sleep, symbolically, when we undergo certain mental disturbances that result in the ephemeral artifacts we call dreams. *The Sound of the Sea* is a dreamy picture and also a nightmare vision. The permanent conundrum of the "nuclear" family is evident here, in a time when we seem to have, at least temporarily, solved more large-scale "nuclear" threats. "Happy" families are almost satisfying, almost fulfilling, almost everything we need. There's always just a little something not quite right, a little something missing. Let's buy a second home at the beach, and then we'll be happy! But in the confrontation of infinity (as represented by the sky and sea) with the nuclear family, every wish comes true except happiness, and no one hears the sea. And if they did, what would it sound like, or mean, or suggest? If this were a practical problem, like plumbing, we'd figure out how to get it fixed. As if everything that we apply our minds to solving, we can handle, but we do our utmost to ignore the question of how to meaningfully deal with each other, or else we are deafened by the noise of our clangingly awkward relationships, and the result is wildly extravagant and beautiful isolation, like the dangerous depths of the sea, and its hidden, destructive power, when it comes to the frail humans that we are and our seemingly grand creations that can be washed away so easily and nonchalantly by a force of nature that neither knows, cares, or notices.

There are desires that get established so early in our lives that we can't recognize them. There are desires that show up later, after becoming so deep-seated that we can't escape them. Some desires are with us every moment, as if we live at the edge of something, and we hear the desire breathing in and out, in and out, all the time, as unrelenting as the ocean. Sometimes a strong desire is associated with simple safety. We want to be protected during anticipated danger, whether physical or emotional. I know my boss will be evaluating me on Monday, and I am full of worry and desire. The worry is about possible negative consequences; the desire is to prepare, perform, triumph, and ultimately be released from the tension and suspense of the coming crisis. *The View* shows us the finest safety, security, and promise of pleasure that money can buy. This kind of "view" of the world is a built-in, dominant desire.

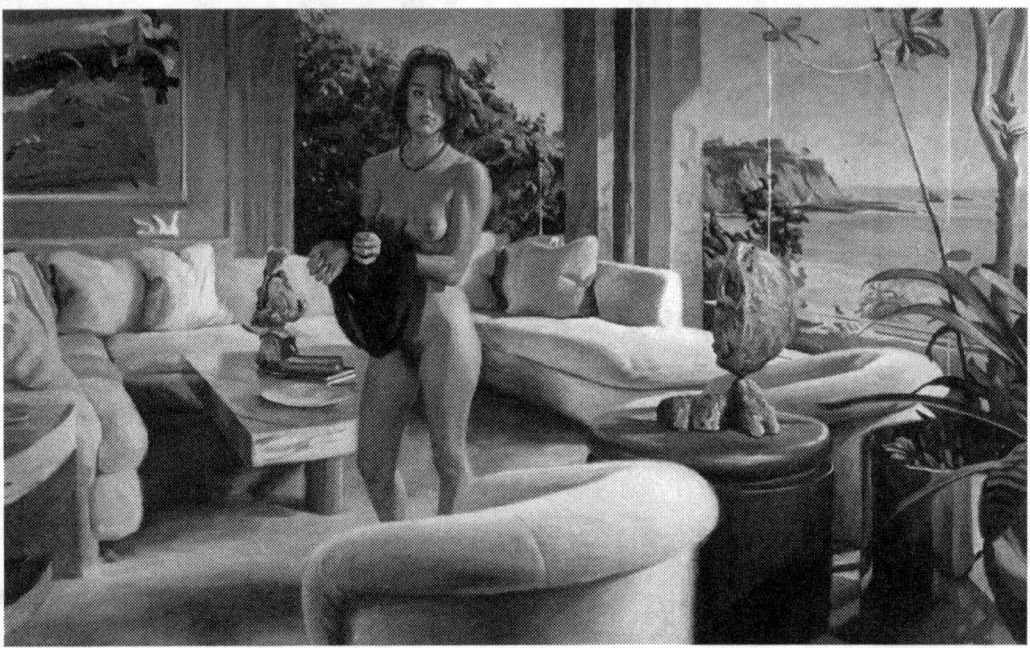

Fig. 10. *The View* (1996, 72" x 119")

The particular view depicted in this painting is clearly an expensive coast, apparently at the edge of an ocean, probably the Pacific. The beauty and agony of isolation is suggested, and the inevitable failure to civilize the edge of the world and all of its primitive qualities. The infinite possibility of nature, or the infinite universe, is completely contained and thwarted. The naked figure could be (or should be) on a nude beach, but it is caged, contained. There is a contrast of the half-shaded column (just on the figure's right) to the cliffs and the horizon to the right of that; the eye keeps going back and forth between the near and the far. Everything looks to be completely firm and solid and enduring, and yet there's something blank about all of this that mirrors the expression on the woman's face. The searing light, the strong vertical presence, and the amplitude of the space doesn't quite reflect the complete beauty of the place that it, by all rights, should. This magnificent place is all for nought. All this lushness is captured, civilized, and overdetermined— she and nature (framed and trapped and captured by the window)—and though she is so "natural," she seems resigned to her captivity, and it ends up stripping her of her naturalness, until she becomes vapid, lifeless, and sterile as a zoo animal. We are all trapped by the material cage we inhabit. We can't get out because we never think to; we don't think of it because we can't perceive the invisible bars that incarcerate us.

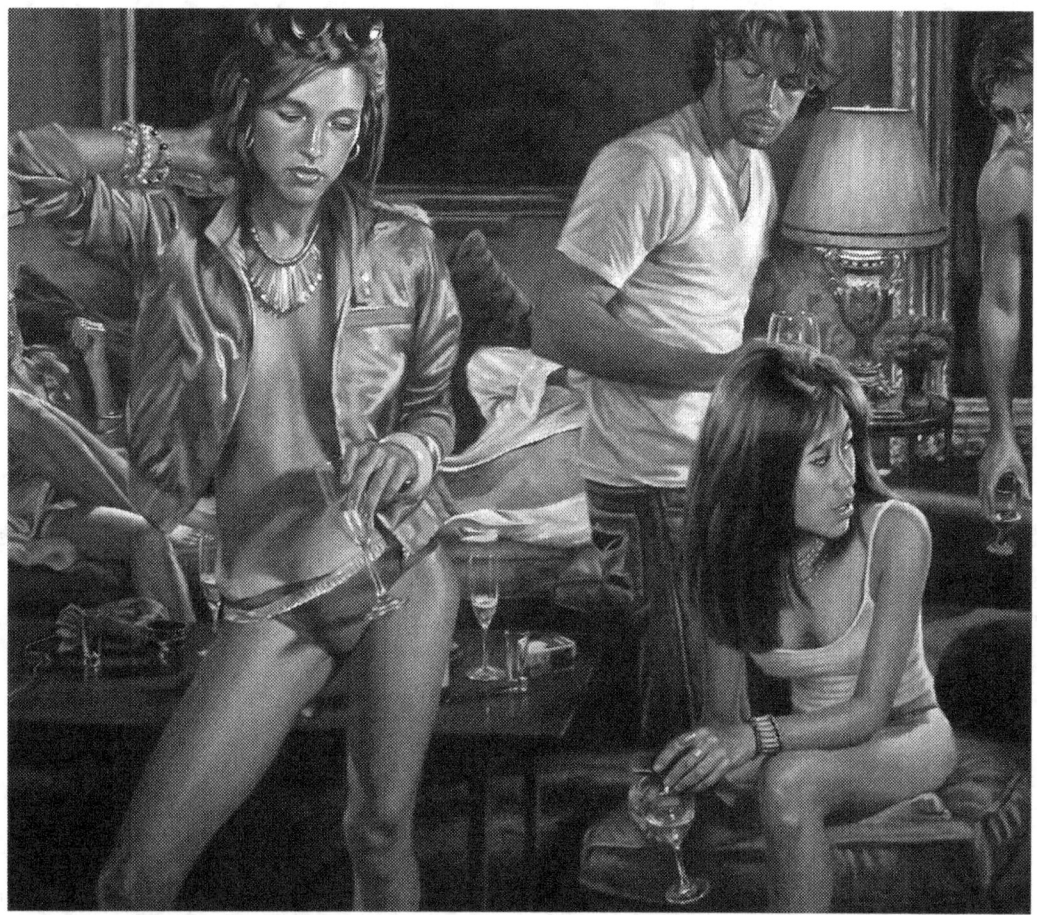

Fig. 11. *A Silver Lining* (2003, 50" x 58 ½")

For all of that, Rodgers still offers us *A Silver Lining* in the cloud that ominously hangs over the new American millennium. Although smaller than many of the recent paintings, *A Silver Lining* nevertheless embodies Rodger's dynamic genius. The elbow of the female figure on the left sends us right out of the picture, but her hand and hip send us even more forcibly back into the frame toward "Brian," who appears in several recent pictures. To have that black painting on the wall, in such a frame, is so interesting, not to mention the enormity of the frame on right. The social environment is half the picture, and there's nothing at all cool about the environment (although it may be hip). The red heats it up, and the gold frames, with all their reddish glows, heat it up further. It's lush and opulent, not over-the-top, but refined and rarified. Nothing is underdone. It represents a certain amount of wealth and taste. Kandinsky, meditating on "the spiritual in art," quotes Delacroix: "Everyone knows that yellow, orange, and red suggest ideas of joy and plenty." But Rodgers employs colors like weapons—sharp-edged ones that cut, and explosive ones that startle us.

In *A Silver Lining*, there is a slightly daring or innovative taste, a combination that is a little uncommon, obviously put together for some kind of "show." None of these people seem to own this place—they're probably too young to have it designed or afford it. Most likely, they would be offspring of the owner, boyfriend-girlfriend, or invitees to some function or activity that the owner has been involved in. It's evidently late in the night, and they didn't get out of their cars or cabs or trains like this. Something's been going on for awhile. There are lots of possibilities. All of that is the background for the three people in the foreground, negotiating some kind of relating in a world without want. Having everything absolutely available does not actually make the people available, or provide them with what they're seeking; and what they look like is not in fact where their heads are. The interior-exterior dichotomy that Rodgers favors is very obvious, with the luscious surfaces that are place and people, the maze in which their heads operate, as if they're individual fish being bandied about by a whirlpool of water, caught in this flux. Something about the energy of this painting suggests that they're getting washed around in it, pushing and pulling in all different directions, as if there is a storm of forces. As static as the faces seem to be, they're under the influence of push and pull, including the black void, and under the influence of vectors of energy, as represented by hands, arms, belts, shadows, torquing. The faces are static and locked and yet completely active, even the restful girl in the far left background, everything going in different directions, static and active.

The black artwork is a surprising symbol of peace in the middle of all of the other meaning-making, meaningless activity. This unapologetic darkness is the locus of resolution or fulfillment, completely void-like and undefined, yet still a symbol for a kind of resolution in this indeterminacy, or even nothingness. In the case of the two figures on the couch, we can't see their faces, so we can't resolve anything about them, which is unsettling. The black panel offers the only sense of peace and takes away everything that make us un- or inhuman. Complete peace would be death. Even that which is false has more richness than the colorless void. People are engaging, upsetting, and rich as hell, endlessly rich—emotionally, physically, mentally—but the black peace is restful, transcendent nothingness. The woman in the frozen fashion pose is runway-like in her attitude, but she's at least present to something going on. There is some language within which she operates, and she's thinking and unsatisfied, perhaps supremely solipsistic. She embodies the desire to be desired. What that can make us do! We calculate "cool" and manipulate our own behaviors and looks in order to see ourselves through the theoretical desires of another, or others, or the wide world. The desire to be desired spawns complex calculations. The vectors are added and subtracted, and the forces are reflected and refracted. But to be desired too much is also a problem. Some people find themselves bombarded and oppressed by the vectors of others' desire.

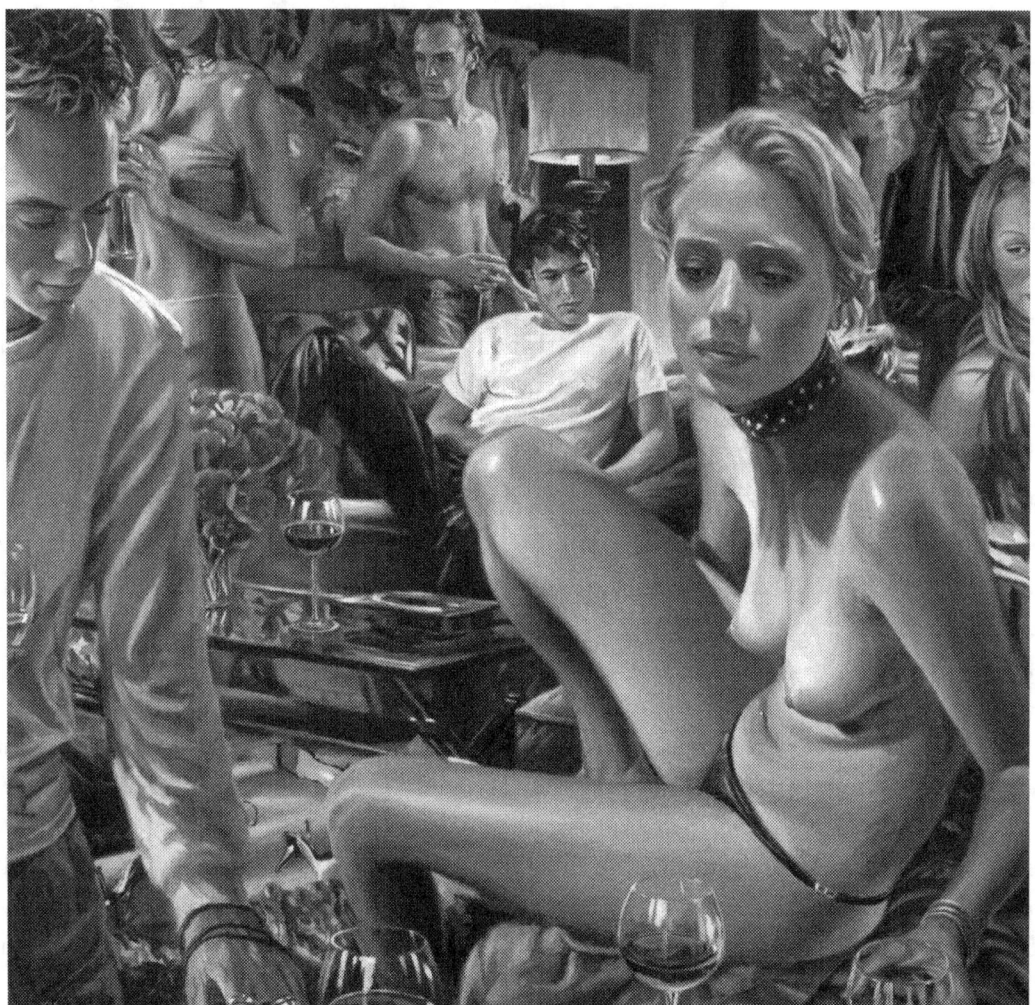

Fig. 12. *Beaujolais Nouveau* (2003, 62" x 66")

Beaujolais Nouveau presents one such vulnerable central character whose chief desire appears to be to leave the scene. Her majestic head ("Eve" again) sails serenely away even as she resides as solidly as a great rock at the center of whatever it is that is happening. Rising above it all, her essence seems to reside outside the scene. The model, almost by definition, is the one who is really not there. She is the model for all of us, the representative person, stuck, but not staying put, in contemporary life. Given our frenetic mobility, always restlessly on the move or connected to someone not physically present, we are never actually anywhere at all. In a culture of excess, the ease of having our basic desires so easily satisfied, and then renewed and satisfied again, causes us to be in perpetual motion and constant emotional turmoil. To be too much the object of desire, on the other hand, is to have many vectors aimed in one's direction, many to fend off, and too little opportunity to send one's own out in directions of one's own choosing. The title suggests the latest new batch of some product that will be quickly consumed. Each year, there is another sparkling, delicious, very affordable crop of young, gorgeous people. For one brief moment in time, they feel that they don't really have to compete, that the world is quite ready, willing, and even eager to offer them whatever they please to take. But then there will be a chilling moment of realization: they will not be new and young and fresh and "perfect" for very long. The next "nouveau" will soon appear, rendering them slightly used consumables, if not entirely obsolete. If they last long enough, they will learn the patient lessons of the ancients (or merely the ancient).

In *Beaujolais Nouveau* and *All About Eve*, the same figure appears, nearly naked, as if akin to the holy men of India, having foresworn the things of this world, willing to be gawked at. They live in a world in which "friends with benefits" and "fuck buddies" are unremarkable categories of acquaintance. Their world doesn't allow them to be in love with anyone in particular. They are exiled from each other and held captive by emotions and secrets and untold (because un-narratable) stories. The power of their desire is bottled up. What have people historically made out of the energy of desire? Ornamental things: cathedrals, and lace, and fables. Nowadays, we make phone calls and send instant messages; we strike poses and transmit digital images to distant screens. Everything is fragmentary. Our behavior is a sequence of self-monitored deletions, after which the only thing left, usually hesitant and timid, is the action we dare not take, and our frightened passivity is perhaps barely noticeable in a world dominated by dramatic and powerful images of assertive, daring, reckless, extravagant personalities. These famous persons are inevitably ruined by their desire, and the media frenzy attending their ruin is like a funeral pyre. Because they are in love with a blossoming and dying culture that feeds on itself, they become martyrs to this high-profile non-cause, to something amoral that is too tender, delicate, and perishable to be articulated, too simple-minded to be believed.

In the context of a culture that seems to be racing toward catastrophe, the most pure and simple fact the paintings communicate is that Rodgers is concerned with humanity in the flesh and in the spirit—and that what he sees in people is primarily their sense of something lacking, and their struggle to somehow make up for it, which translates to what we call "desire," for lack of a better word, with all of its confusing sources, forces, and directions. The artist often sets aside the question of healthy or sick desire to focus on his view that, because we share the human condition, we all succumb to patterns, habits, compulsions, obsessions, addictions. Even our most constructive habits can become, over time, destructive. To be born with self-consciousness and imagination, and to educate these faculties and nourish them and exercise them, is to have a terminal spiritual illness aggravated by a chronic emotional discomfort. But there is always the choice, however unappealing: one could ignore all of this. One might want to escape from the scenes Rodgers shows, but all of that is just too "cool" to seriously consider giving up. By reasoning that we shouldn't miss out on the experience, we blind ourselves to the sacrifice we make. To give in is to be a part of the scene, and when we leave the scene we feel that somehow we are not in the center of what is happening. The lights and colors and people and objects are not as bright and interesting. Everything else is proverbially "pale by comparison."

In 1975, Bob Dylan's *Desire* liner notes declared, "Romance is taking over." After the Vietnam nightmare, fantasy of any kind seemed preferable to reality. Or perhaps, in the wake of the Carter years, it was mere excess that looked attractive. In any case, the vulgar reality at large is often an invitation to make-believe, to anything verging on the romantic. Rodgers' scenes show the continuing reign of the myth of the romantic in several modes, principally in fashion, furniture, architecture, and even the club scene. Rodgers' people are trapped in clothing, settings, attitudes, and groups, and wrapped in unexamined desire. Their only possible escape—counterfeited freedom—is through the vehicle of conscious and even reckless desire. And yet they all seem so careful. To plunge headlong into love is to author and authorize a fantastic creative accomplishment, a kind of free-floating, histrionic mystery of the very soul of which one is simultaneously the sorcerer source and the helpless victim. But these people Rodgers creates, who are apparently not in love, seem fundamentally undisturbed in their souls, merely restless in their senses and motives. They are hesitant, reluctant, calculating, holding as much as possible in reserve: holding back everything they can.

Desire can be a sick thing, an addiction, a compulsion, an obsession, or a simple, sad yearning for something to be or not to be. There must be some combination of pills and herbal remedies to cure these maladies; if only we could have the right thoughts. We have dozens of new disorders and syndromes and diseases. We have desires to know what is wrong with us and how to get it fixed. We can have cosmetic surgery, personal trainers, injections of things. When one's life is in actual, palpable danger, desire can be at its most basic and forceful: simply the urge to keep on living, to continue to be alive, to struggle through whatever threatens to not let us simply be. If we could only remember to simply *be* when we have the ephemeral luxury of feeling unthreatened! Desire can be a pure and healthy thing; it can be the essence of life itself. The natural growth of young things is desire in its most pure and formidable form, movement from some small, known spot towards something much larger—something impossible to know.

3. A Vectoral Architecture

"It's what makes my pictures different."
—Terry Rodgers

In 1994, Rodgers created two paintings that heralded a new development in his interest and experimentation: *Beach Venus* and *The Ambassador's Son*. *Beach Venus* grew out of the St. Tropez scenes Rodgers had been painting for the previous few years, beginning with his first visit to the nude beaches in 1991. Rodgers then translated the dense mass of naked humanity in the St. Tropez scenes into a completely different setting, the interior scene of *The Ambassador's Son*, in which the figures are not only fully clothed, but in formal dress. It is in these two superficially opposite paintings that Rodgers fully develops his "vectoral" model, a way of seeing and painting which highlights and connects emotional, cultural, and physical dynamics, especially desires (conscious and unconscious). Later still, in the first year of the twenty-first century, and in the aftermath of "9/11," he would bring skin indoors, as it were, and claim for interior scenes the abandoned, yet relaxed ethos of the nude beach, or the subdued, wild-yet-intimate quality of *Elizabeth*, in which the paint itself represents those continuously shifting human forces Rodgers likes to call vectors, where the surface of the subject's skin is moving all the time, as if to represent her own internal reality.

The development of vectors to represent values and forces has been fruitful for math and science, for theoretical activity and for intensely practical matters like air traffic control, where the numberless vectors keep the many thousands of aircraft and millions of passengers from the kind of dangerous confusion that individual humans cannot be protected from. But vectors can also help

43

us understand human thinking and feeling. The idea that there are directional forces at work in our minds and hearts that, when added, subtracted, multiplied and otherwise combined, can actually indicate behaviors, is a hopeful and fascinating one. In Rodgers' recent paintings, these vectors are spatially and symbolically apparent, and they can especially illuminate a particular dimension of human experience: that mysterious, sublime, often obsessive and compulsive, always compelling realm of desire. Vectors involve propulsion, braking, letting go, steering, and forces impinging on us from all sides. Unbridled desire could conceivably take over if we let go and just see where it takes us. But who among us can ever really "let go," except when we orchestrate something artificially intoxicating to take us beyond ourselves. We don't really even know our own desires, except the one that is the great cornerstone of civilization: the desire to be "under control."

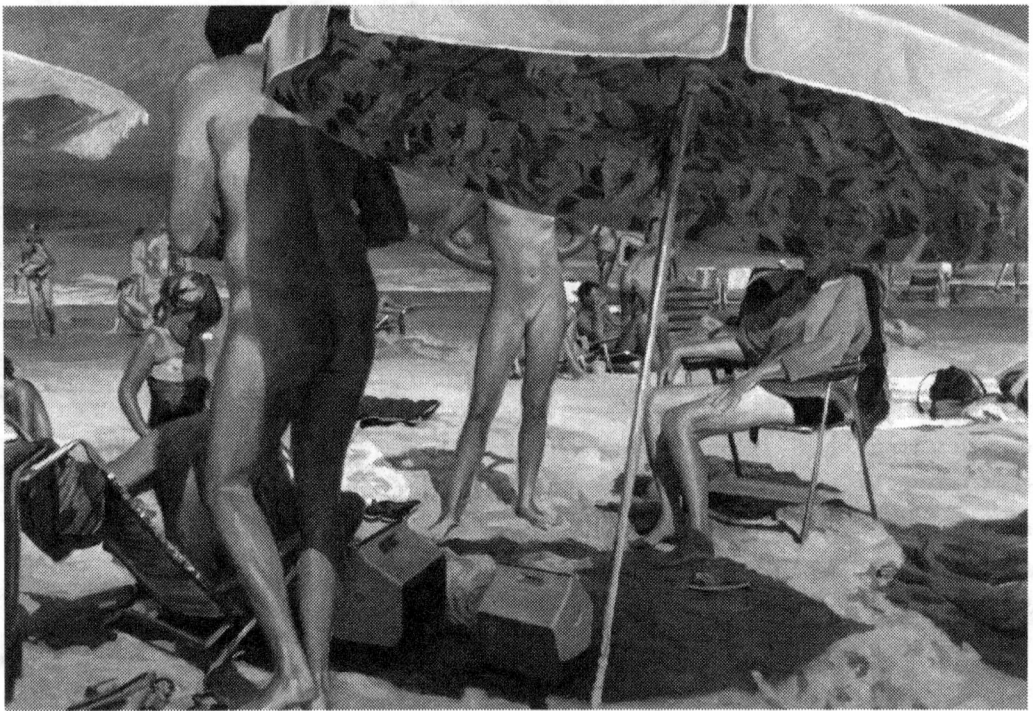

Fig. 13. *Beach Venus* (1994, 60" x 90 ½")

Beach Venus is a fully-realized painting that can be too easily overlooked because it is "pretty" or too-quickly dismissed because it is "naughty." Perhaps because it is so complete, a viewer can pass it by after a few moments and move on, with the sensation of having glimpsed everything at once, consumed the image in a glance. But this painting is about everything and everyone, about birth and death, beginning and end, infinity and the very finite, limited, mortal humanity we think we know so well. It's about everything on the underside of the umbrella, everything, in other words, on the face of this earth, especially our earthbound selves. But the painting goes beyond what we can know. By manipulating sun and shade, Rodgers suggests the good and the bad, the young and the old, the practical and the fantastic, and the result is that, as he puts it, "There is nothing missing in this painting."

We see an array of people. They are not only in the sunshine, the very brilliant sunshine; they are silhouetted against a not very friendly looking sky, with the confusing umbrella, shadowed on the underside and casting its own dark, unnatural, civilizing shadow on a small section of the beach. The sunshine is accented and compromised by all of the shade and the foreboding sky. The earth ends and water begins: the unknown, the bigness, the allness, the nothingness. On the far left, in the distance, near the water, there is a man carrying a very small child. Closer to us on the left, there is a slightly older child under the naked-but-benign large man, probably the father, with the half-hidden seated figure possibly his wife. So we see a mom and a dad, and probably a grandmother in the chair on the right, her legs wasting away. We can observe the entire movement of the human life experience, all the threats that everybody faces from beginning to end. The looming male dominates the scene, his nakedness revealing and highlighting the kind of tan that is the scar of genteel life. Meanwhile, the pubescent title figure, her head cut off by the umbrella, represents the magical, mysterious, and dangerously rapid transition from innocent youth to a young adulthood tainted by a painful self-consciousness in the face of a social spectacle too complex to comprehend. Here is everything that threatens everybody, but all of the threats are marginalized by the margin of the land, from which most of the figures turn away, or stay as far from as possible. Only the title figure is turned fully toward the world of culture. We don't see her face; we see hardly any faces, and it's unsettling. But we do see the growing body that will soon be her ticket into the high-stakes competition that young women are thrust into. With artful coverings (and equally artful uncovering), she will take her place in the "sun" of the social scene. Little does she now know, and little is she ever likely to understand, of the forces that will take her from the innocence of childhood through the years of increasing sophistication and cynicism, and out on the other end to her grandmother's place.

Beach Venus is about everybody and about the difficulty of facing one another, isolated and separate as we are. The large male is three-quarters shadowed; his life is lived in the shadow. The older woman in the chair is perhaps coming to terms with her life, not moving, just watching, waiting, as so many of Rodgers' figures watch and wait, and as the viewer must watch and wait to see the movement in the picture indicated by the careful vectors of gesture and posture and glance. With further study, we can appreciate the energy of the child at the far right, past the lady. And there is the inertia of the stuff sitting on the beach, or simply left there. The world of *Beach Venus* is vast; it is infinite. It is also local, vulnerable, and poignant in its depiction of the mythical nuclear family in an Edenic safe zone. Rodgers will only say, "It's the whole story to me." He has evoked the purest of human desires in this canvas: for food when very hungry, for warmth when very cold, for dryness when very wet, for silence when very loud, for that which we lack. In Rodgers' paintings, there is always the interrogation of personal identity, personal and social space, and individual uniqueness—the persistent problem of sincerity, confidence (or faith), and purpose. "We can make anything happen technologically," he observes, "but we can make nothing happen personally."

The Ambassador's Son marks the other end of the spectrum of Rodgers' subject matter, moving us into the indoor civilization that distances itself from the human body, from nature, and from everything not orderly, clean, and socially acceptable. In fact, the two paintings represent opposing categories, two separate tracks, that are themselves re-configured by the darker "third rail." (Paintings like *The Watchman* and *Between Acts* would be grouped there, which are a combination of the social and the sinister.) *The Ambassador's Son*, with all of its extensive, elaborate, well-lighted social niceties, speaks to the innumerable tensions of the global village, from oppression to condescension, to a now-current and slightly less-objectionable exoticism.

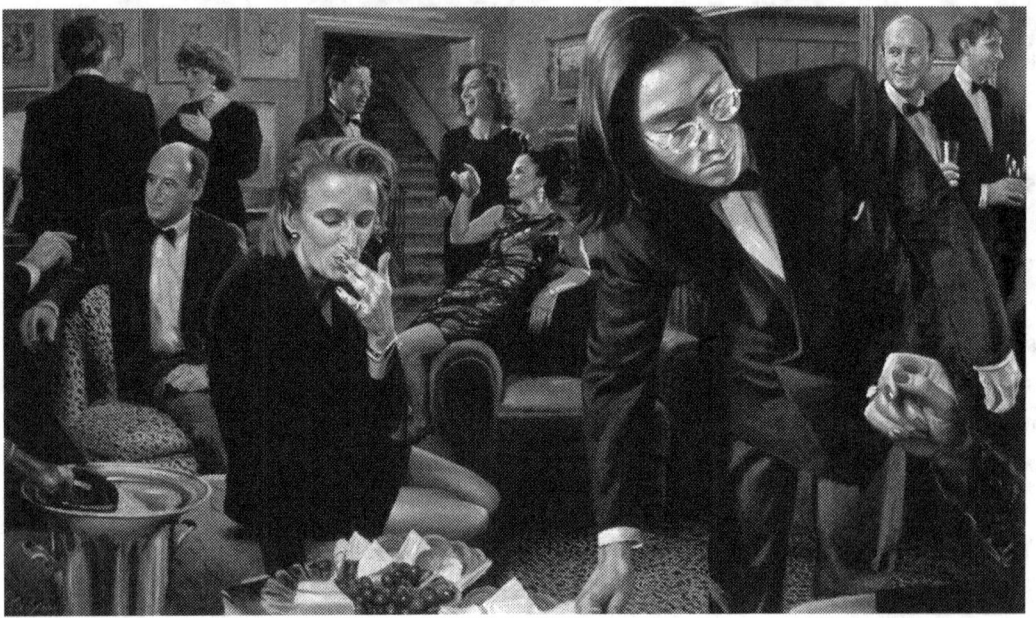

Fig. 14. *The Ambassador's Son* (1994, 54" x 94")

For those who like narratives in their pictures, *The Ambassador's Son* is a meta-narrative. On its surface (and by its title), it strongly suggests an intricate, intimate, incestuous novel that Henry James might have written. But it is also a global narrative, all wrapped up in one picture. It is the history of eroticism and the history of commerce. It is the march of civilization and the brutal quotidian practices of mythological primitive tribes, which could hardly be more violent than our technologically-advanced motor vehicle mass casualties and our highly-organized abortion carnage. In contrast to *Beach Venus*, *The Ambassador's Son* is all about sublimation. In *Beach Venus*, you can't see any faces, but you get what's going on. In *The Ambassador's Son*, you see all the faces, and yet everyone is dissembling, rather than grabbing someone and taking them to task or to bed. This is all about selling real estate and looking cool. *Beach Venus* is naked; nothing is being sold. *The Ambassador's Son* is a masterly cultural attempt to hide what each individual is actually about, not to mention what the culture as a whole is about. The two paintings are a beautiful, sinister contrast. In *The Ambassador's Son*, there are hands everywhere, but six hands that are incredibly telling: reaching out on left, up in center, finger-licking in left center, hand reaching down bottom center, blood-red nails/claws reaching up from right. There is a rhythm of the hands, like some so-called primitive culture's lost rite. The grapes in the center represent appetite: they are an incarnation of pure desire. The empty chair and the black-tie straitjacket represent what is lacking and what is impossible, with all of the constraints so elaborately in operation, and all of the codes of commerce and propriety so much in evidence.

The Ambassador's Son, in the world of Rodgers' work, is the epitome of clothing, furnishing, decoration, and all other forms of covering-up—or cover-ups. And, of course, at its center, with the woman licking her fingers above the little feast, there is a Garden of Eden quality, the innocence that is continually renewed and then every moment turned into corruptive experience. The constant, underlying, buzzing, static-ridden confusion of human beings as innocents and sinners, saints and exploiters, existing in the present moment and being seduced by the glorious hope of a delayed gratification that will win everything: the whole world, what they inherited and were robbed of, by others just like them. Granted, those others may look slightly different and have mannerisms that seem a little odd. It is all about strangeness and familiarity, and of course the contempt of the self-appointed superiors for those whom they've designated as their inferiors. Viewed one way, Rodgers is astonishingly adept at group portraiture; viewed another, these are individual studies that he has fused in a seamless ensemble vision of interlocking forces that we can intuit but never precisely name.

Rodgers frequently speaks of the "simultaneity" of multiple aspects of reality, including the "push-pull" of unlimited forces, opportunities, and desires, "all of it going on and on at the same time." He wants to represent all of this chaos and confusion "without resolving it." His compositions seek forms that will do that. Gerhard Richter was recently quoted in *The New York Times* as saying, in effect, that form is all we have these days: "Form is all we have to help us cope with fundamentally chaotic facts and assaults." Richter speaks of building structures "from dumb abundance," adding, "Whatever is real is so unlimited and unshaped that we have to summarize it" ("A Picture Is Worth 216 Newspaper Articles," July 4, 2004).

In terms of the force of form versus the power of paint itself, Rodgers remembers seeing Manet's *A Bunch of Asparagus* and feeling the revelation of the duality of experiencing two things at once, "this absolute slurry of paint and this actual asparagus." This breakthrough experience with "the abstraction of realism" was the embryonic sensation that led to Rodgers seeing vectors everywhere and trying to represent them. "It dawned on me then that one of the integral parts of the magic of painting and art in general is this back-and-forthness." It's what he is primarily preoccupied with in his own work to this day, and the techniques Rodgers employs are very effective in generating a dialectical tension in the paintings, and at the same time they allow him to make the most of his brushwork, celebrating the pleasures of the paint. The spatial, emotional, and painterly dynamics are complex and powerful; they grow on us as we stand in front of a painting.

Rodgers enjoys speaking of the "vectors" and "vectoring" in his paintings, and one doesn't have to look far to see where the concept comes from. A voracious and ambitious reader, the painter is an enormous fan of David Foster Wallace, whose novel *Infinite Jest* early on speaks of the vectors in a room. In many of Rodgers' best paintings, as the painter likes to say, "everything bounces off everything else." The effect is not narrative, not even situational, it is "vectoral." It is about connectivity and the vectors of connectivity, visually, psychologically, conceptually, and ideologically. It is about the idea of the "knowable" running up against the "unknowable," and the feeble "intentional" human world colliding with the much more solid and unyielding "unintentional." Rodgers uses his concept of vectoring as a natural meta-force, of which gravity and light are the two greatest sub-categories.

"You look at a lot of paintings and you can extrapolate a story or situation, but I don't look at this as a room, but rather as a 'happening.'" Rodgers told me, speaking of *This Is Our Youth*. "Part of it is this funny thing between the big, physical immediacy of the central figure or 'leading lady'—her hands and breasts and lips—and the interior life implied. So we go back and forth between the luscious and detailed outside and the poignant interior, and we go back and forth from her bigness in the front of the painting to the more distant and smaller figures throughout the painting. And with each of them, we go inside-outside. It's a war in our attention between the seductive exterior and their overwhelming details. And the concerns of the individuals that these exteriors tend to distract us from. So my sense about the painting is that we find ourselves constantly wanting to look at the details of, say, the figure in the bottom right corner—her face, hair, breast, necklace—all the surface things, and ask what that has to do with her inner experience, which is so loudly implied in her face. Or what does it have to do with our own experience? Which may actually be obvious in our faces as we take in the painting. We all—I'm including the figures in the painting—are seduced by the exteriors, by surface beauty, or money, possessions, breasts, abs, faces."

Vectors can be used to represent any force/motion/direction. They apply so well to Rodgers because of all the potential energy that is palpable in his paintings: the actual and symbolic forces, as well as the obvious and hidden ones. Vectors can re-direct; vectors can add and subtract. One can get "vectored around" by forces beyond one's control until one is going in exactly the opposite direction. One can be, like a commercial aircraft, vectored into a holding pattern, which is simply a continual re-vectoring, with the practical effect of getting in or on line, queuing up in order to reach a destination desired by the many, perhaps even the masses. Vectors can be calculated to intersect and intercept, to meet and join. Vectors can result in collisions, at a focal point or before it. We can put ourselves in parallel paths and move together in the same direction. The vector is not the force or the thing itself, but only a way to plot, represent, indicate, trace, imagine, project, follow, understand, comprehend, calculate, map, predict, influence (perhaps, by steering or calibrating).

With any Rodgers painting of the past fifteen years, the notion of multiple presences of dynamic and complex vectors provides a way to read the painting. Not that the paintings are narrative, but that they are in some sense alive. The manifold human desires are present in the paintings, and they can be located in the various vectoral forces associated with the torquing of a posture, the turn of a head, the angle of an arm, or the intensity of a glance. Even the angles of light, shadow, furniture, and floor add their perspectival vectors to the dazzling effects of the human energies Rodgers captures in what appear at first glance to be perfectly fixed, micro-second snapshots or elaborately-designed, artificial tableaux.

In her 1963 Foreword to *Tropisms*, Nathalie Sarraute identifies a primal and prototypical human moment that she associates with childhood, a moment of essential authenticity, a pure experience of being that is dynamic. It seems to capture in words what Rodgers gets at in his brilliant portraits of the individual adrift in the larger world, packed in among others, with everything arranged to highlight artificiality and all but eliminate the simple, unique quality that defines each of us. Sarraute descries "movements": "These movements, of which we are hardly cognizant, slip through us on the frontiers of consciousness in the form of undefinable, extremely rapid sensations. They hide behind our gestures, beneath the words we speak, the feelings we manifest, are aware of experiencing, and able to define. They...seem to me to constitute the secret source of our existence, in what might be called its nascent state." Sarraute, discussing her attempts to communicate such moments in prose, goes on to say this: "Time was no longer the time of real life, but of a hugely amplified present." This is the moment that Rodgers captures, "the hugely amplified present," and in that moment he tries to show us the forces that are always at work, and the web that is always connecting everything.

Connection and Light

Rodgers' achievement would be formidable if we only attended to the effects he realizes with light. Some figures and objects are bathed in it, some are hiding from it, and, everywhere in between, the magic of light touches the likenesses Rodgers has rendered. By following the flow of light in any Rodgers painting, we can extract a whole story in itself, the narrative of illumination and mystery that is purely sensual. Rodgers sometimes seems to make light the primary subject of his work. By following the varying shadows, we see the characters in "a new light." We can see what they can see in the space in which they are caught, among the faces and objects.

Rodgers could say, as Richter has, "The central problem of my painting is light." Like Richter did later in his career, Rodgers has also taken on the "problem" of light as one of his central themes. There are very light and very dark areas in the paintings, creating a sun and shadow effect that draws the eye and the mind to questions of behavior and meaning. Like Richter, too, Rodgers has been concerned with realism and abstraction, and, relatedly, with photography and painting. Rodgers makes everything work for him; unlike Richter, he has committed himself to a recognizably consistent and ever-evolving approach. What is remarkable about Rodgers' work is that, in the limits of the repetition and serialization of the imagery, he continues, as does Richter, to offer delight and insight without resorting to gimmickry, or trickery, or experimentation for experimentation's sake.

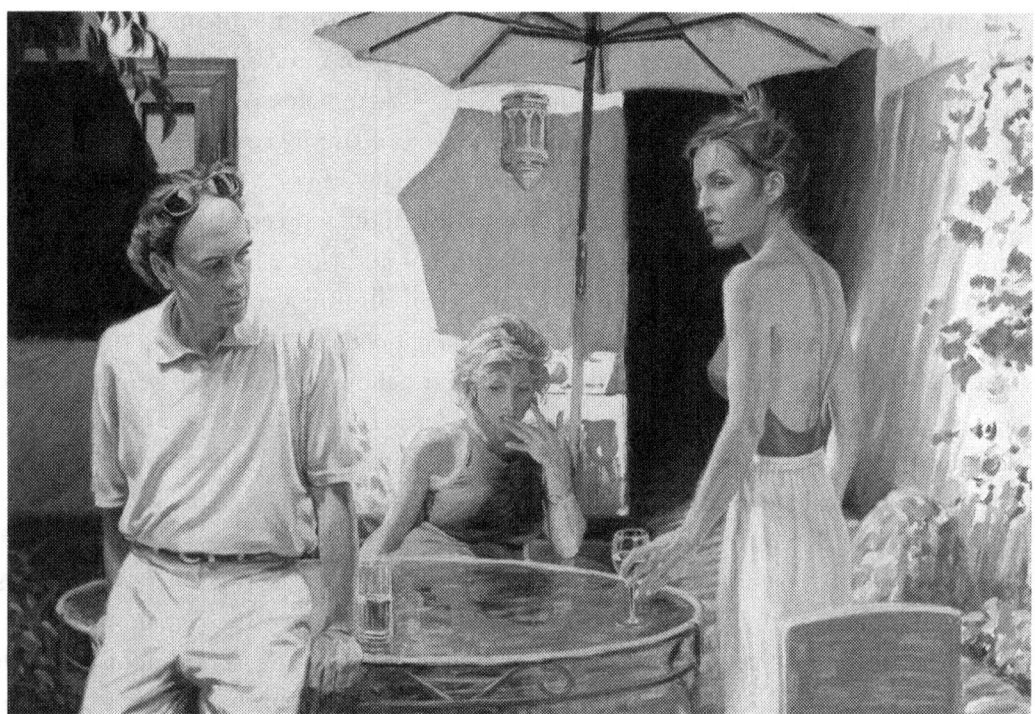

Fig. 15. *The Opacity of Light* (2001, 48" x 72")

Like Richter, too, Rodgers loves to "look at looking." *The Opacity of Light* is a study of the mystery and illumination of obviousness and despair. Here is an unmanageable *ménage a trois*, in a place that could well be California, which, despite decades of hype, never did prove to be a state of grace. (Once one attains California, the idea of grace quickly goes by the boards.) It's a picture about three people struggling either in isolation or in communication, with brilliant light shining down on everything about them. There are impenetrable dark places into which you cannot see for all the light. It remains unknowable. There is a rhythmic circle of incompletion, which seems to be a circular pool of water, reflecting them and their world and the whole thing circling 1-2-3, 1-2-3, 1-2-3, dark places, for all the light, no resolution. The vectors twist their bodies toward and away in powerful torquing. The bold brushstrokes go sideways in the table and chair.

This is a very adult painting, a narrative that no one wants to be involved in, and yet one that adults all seem to have too much experience with. It is about the threat of betrayal, about the imminence of an undermining suspicion, about dishonesty that destroys pleasures no one wanted to address in language. Everything is in the light now, even if it isn't articulated in so many words.

To distinguish between legitimate and natural desires and illegitimate, unnatural desires is perhaps no longer possible. The idea of "natural" is itself an impossibly complex construct. We are lost once we try to find ourselves by ourselves. All that remains is a choice of which community of persons we wish to join, and then, from them, we can simply consider the menu of desires that are available and appropriate (and try to forget about the others).

In interior scenes like *This Is Our Youth*, the visible light sources are multiple and complex (two lamps, seven candles, and a fire), but it is obvious that additional light sources are located high on the walls or on the ceiling, unseen, but with their illumination fully rendered in angle and intensity. By contrast, in *The Opacity of Light*, Rodgers floods the scene with a single source of light, but it is a scene that remains impenetrable. The light shows too much; it shows too little. It's not that the participants could possibly be dull or dense, except in some emotionally disabled or disconnected sense. The twisted and misdirected postures and glances tell a story of troubled, baffled, or paralyzing desire. The vectors of the eyes and bodies create a swirling effect, a vortex common to many Rodgers compositions.

It's possible that the diurnal banality of their lives has been captured here, but it's also possible that some emotional catastrophe has occurred. The position of the female figure on the right directs the eye to the man on the left, whose large forehead suggests thought, difficult thought, unpleasant, uneasy, and unfulfilling. The sunglasses perched on his head suggest blank eyes gazing heavenward, in search of some answer for this earthbound mortal. Like the glasses on his head, the man's body is perched on the edge of the table, temporarily, and delicately. There is nothing solid or permanent. His back is to the seated central female figure in the low background, but his body twists incompletely toward the other female figure, as if in a tentative attempt to connect that has been thought better of. For her part, the seated female is protected and trapped. She seems to be lost in her own private reflections or fears, and in those she is almost safe, fingers to her mouth, perhaps finding a hint of remembered sweetness on her fingertips. But she is also captive in the situation, blocked in, framed and caged by the other two. The standing woman on the right seems to be turned toward the male figure, but her gaze goes past his head into some indefinite beyond, where perhaps there is a safer and saner place for her. The big blank space of the sun-drenched white wall is emblematical of the emptiness of the scene. It suggests love going wrong from the point of view of the one losing: one can't believe it when it's happening, like some terrible catastrophe, whether a car crash or earthquake or explosion, but worse, because it's only personal and individual, not distributed among a large number of people.

In *The View*, the light catches the single female figure's naked hip in the same way that it catches the furniture, rendering her just so much human furniture in this light, in this setting. In one sense, she seems to belong, but by studying her face we learn otherwise. Her expression is uneasy, tentative, as if she is expecting to be asked to leave. Someone, almost certainly not this woman, has assembled this elaborate setting, and incorporated nature (and her) into it in an extravagant, elaborate, but ultimately empty manner. Rodgers' observation of such a scene shows us that the superficial beauty of the construct is also riddled with flaws. The gaps between what we call "reality" (our perceived "actual" experience) and the myths through which we interpret the world are very large, and they make for both hazardous and interesting effects, creating tension and confusion that colors our lives, whether we know it or not. In many of the paintings, Rodgers seems to be looking at the interactions (and non-interactions) within a particular stratum of American society, examining individuals in their uncomfortably affluent environment, and pointing to the gaping holes in the situation that, on first glance, seems desirable. Surrounded by symbols of lives well-lived, Rodgers' characters (they are in a sense fictional creations more than amateur or professional models posing and posed) explore how the myths of idealism and perfectibility clash with the so-called reality of present experience. When ordinary gestures and faces are seen up close, hope and fear don't take the shape of demons or distorted, contorted figures. It would be easier if they did. Instead, they fester, cloy, appall, or seduce in the very familiar, therefore contemptible quarters of our daily lives. Though these paintings can be read as metaphor, the figures are not meant as icons or symbolic forms. Rodgers creates authentic human beings, and the situations he puts them in, if indeterminate, are always unnervingly complex in their possibilities.

The much-touted symbols of American success and mastery have no bearing on the difficulties we experience with each other and within ourselves. Rodgers is interested in what lies behind this facade of success, and he offers hints through the vector of light itself. A close examination of the bright and dark spaces, and the seemingly insignificant details of the faces and gestures, reminds us of just how much of our mental life is disguised and sublimated. By carefully orchestrating the vectoral structure, Rodgers suggests the physical interconnectedness of all the parts, in the hope of making more obvious the intricate web of the unseen and unspoken. By creating very large figures, he virtually places the viewer within the composition, and invites the viewer to participate (almost demands it, really) in the complex negotiation of social surface and psychological depth. And it is in the interplay of silences and gestures, the careful delineation of what we think we can see, as well as what we can't, that these works offer unsettling meditations on isolation, loss and, in the end, opportunities to make our own brand of meaning, just like our cultural heroes and heroines, who have in fact branded themselves: they are famous for being exactly who they are.

Regarding Rodgers' awareness and playful manipulation of Christian religious themes (as in *Cross Currents*), it is interesting to note Alan Watts in *Myth and Ritual in Christianity* (132): "In so far as we are aware of life as history only, as a series of facts, the life that we know is an abstraction without real value or joy. This will include our specious 'present,' which is not the true present but a memory of the immediate past—the so-called *nunc fluens* as distinguished from the *nunc stans*, the present which is always flying away as distinct from that which is eternal." Compare David Foster Wallace's more-fun-to-seek-than-have observation from Alcoholics Anonymous with Watts' observation about Western Culture's frantic character: "It is a desperate rush in pursuit of ever-receding 'meaning,' because the promising future is precisely the famous carrot which the clever rider dangles before the donkey's nose from the end of his whip."

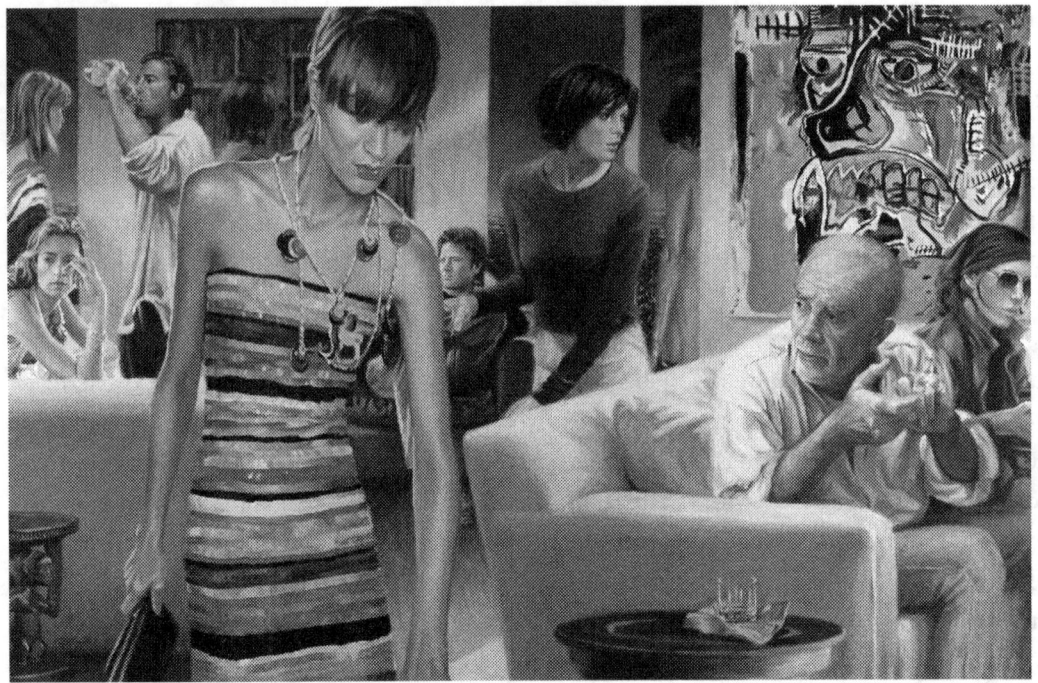

Fig. 16. *Rewriting the Book* (2001, 54" x 84")

Rewriting the Book speaks to the persistence of American hopefulness that never gives up re-fantasizing the failed dream, re-calibrating the secular faith. In some ways, this painting calls attention to Rodgers' entire project of investigating the ways that we construct meaning from our own fantastic imaginations, but often in a vulgar manner that reduces human creativity to the material minimum and short-circuits the most profound desires that could otherwise lead our thought and behavior to more interesting places. This painting, with its obviously voyeuristic older man, highlights the way we use other people for our own limited ends. Perhaps he needs to observe a young woman simply to assuage the outrage of his antiquity, to grant him a momentary reprieve from his own sense of being *passé*, or to steal some energy from an involuntary muse. Whatever his motivation, his apparently calculating manner renders him so much less sympathetic than the completely exposed and honest old age of the man in *Timepiece*. In a larger sense, *Rewriting the Book* points to the ways we navigate through the signs of our cultural present, trying to find a niche, or rehabilitate the niche we occupy, trying to keep up with the surging new information that always threatens to render us obsolete.

The fictions we create to live within at the turn of a new millennium (and, in this case, before the apotheosis of terrorism embodied by "9/11") can be seen in what it takes in Los Angeles (in Hollywood, more specifically—or perhaps it should be "more generally"?) to be successful. First, people dress for the party, wearing head scarves, a designer multi-color print tube dress, or, like the guy in the back, whatever his mode of dressing indicates (maybe it says "writer" or "director"). Whoever owns the house makes it available for a get-together like this and puts paintings on the walls that define him as being right up there with the best of them. The suggestion is that it creates a rarefied atmosphere and yet for all of the fictive inventiveness it remains rather sterile, and the internal energies (vectors) reflected in the Basquiat painting on the right have been refined, processed, and converted into something like the dress this woman is wearing.

The central action of the painting is of course in the mind of the older man, who is apparently engaged in making something out of the many somethings that have been made by the woman he studies. He seems to be taking ideas from her, things that he needs in order to revise his own aging concepts and projects. Just as we make something of the painting, he makes something of the construct that is her, just as she makes something of the hair, jewelry, dress, perfume, and whatever else she is employing in the service of the image she has of herself, in this innocent and corrupt cultural moment that now, with a few more years of hindsight, looks so privileged in its naïve and yet blatant confidence. As if there were nothing to do those few short years ago but to study how we might make something even more prepossessing out of our personalities, appearances, and projects. And, in fact, how little our circumstances and attitudes have changed since "9/11." If anything, judging by Rodgers' more recent works, we have become more extravagant in our desire to have a personal impact, especially in the face of our fears and fantasies of terror.

After we get acclimated to the universe of Rodgers' paintings, we see our own world through the models' faces and through the models' eyes. Real people and real professional models are his models, but, once they become part of a painting, they become our models, whether of something we wish to emulate or avoid. Rodgers exploits this transference in explicit terms. In every sense, he makes the most of his models, and, as a matter of fact, he is photographing models most of the time. His phenomenally productive painting output of the past few years has been directly tied to a steady stream of models he photographs wherever he can get them to pose for him, for sixty seconds or sixty minutes, in the street or in a restaurant or department store, in his home or in his studio, amateurs and professionals alike. His pleasure in working among people is reminiscent of something the novelist John Fowles poignantly expressed when he watched the making of the movie of his novel, *The French Lieutenant's Woman*. To be alone and work the way a novelist must work in his study—or a painter in his studio—is to be deprived of the social side of a vocation. But Rodgers does not deprive himself of the social possibilities of his creative efforts. He visibly draws energy from his models, and shoots dozens (and sometimes hundreds) of digital images of each one.

Although he has used scores of inexperienced amateurs, Rodgers frequently finds professional models in seemingly improbable ways. But, as he puts it, "It's really no accident, because I recognize what made them professional models the moment I see them." Amateur or professional, it matters nothing to Rodgers, who is dedicated to seeing something in a face or figure that he can paint. With Robert Henri, Rodgers might say, "A good model is one whose lines have meaning" (*The Art Spirit* 245). Rodgers pores over his rows of digital images of a recent shoot in the hope of finding a single photograph that shows him the line of a back or jaw or leg that he wants to paint. So, too, with Henri, Rodgers might say, "The model is not to be copied, but to be realized. The painting is the result of the effect of the model on the artist. It is not the model we need but the vision."

Increasingly, celebrity models are becoming for many of us the vision of what we want to be: celebrated, wealthy, with entry everywhere. Instead of something to test or show the fit of clothing, models have become "super"; we see them as something above the ordinary human status, larger than life, and it is no accident because they are taller and thinner and younger than most people who model themselves after them. In fact, in Rodgers' vision, the celebrity is one of the most powerful social vectors of our time. In the bright light of publicity, the person playing the role of the one whom everyone is supposed to desire and envy becomes a possible direction for us. Are we drawn to be near them, or shall we merely imitate them; do we want to be close or merely a close approximation? This is a continual force that draws us out of ourselves, that causes us to consider re-drawing our own self-portraits and boundaries and dreams. These days, when young people "see the light," more often than not it is the bright light of some perishable celebrity. Everything points to where we are not.

4. The Vectors of Desire

*"If, at any moment, we find we're not wanting something,
we want to be wanting something."*
—Terry Rodgers

In *Anatomy of Desire*, as in *Shades of Olympus*, Rodgers presents a party scene featuring Paris Hilton. To be at a party with a famous person is to become, by extension, significant. One is illuminated in one's own mind by the proximity of the shimmering one. Paris Hilton who, at this writing, is famously "famous for being famous," serves as the ultimate empty container of our fantasies about significance. She represents fame, celebrity, notoriety, or even simple name-and-face recognition in this time of so many famous people and so little lasting significance to what can loosely be called their achievements. To be someone who knows someone or has been with someone or who has seen someone is somehow, if fleetingly, significant. We go to a concert and we say that we have "seen" Pavarotti or Dylan or Madonna. And, by extension, we have been seen with them. But when we do not pay to "see" them but actually lend our presence to an event in the same simple way that the celebrity does, there is a heightening of the tension in our head. We are somewhere, we are someone, but the something significant we feel because of it is merely owing to the coincidence of presences. Ultimately, for the purposes of valuation, Paris Hilton is not just a person but a thing, an ornament and emblem of a volatile culture that transforms itself continually in order to mask the essential absence at its core.

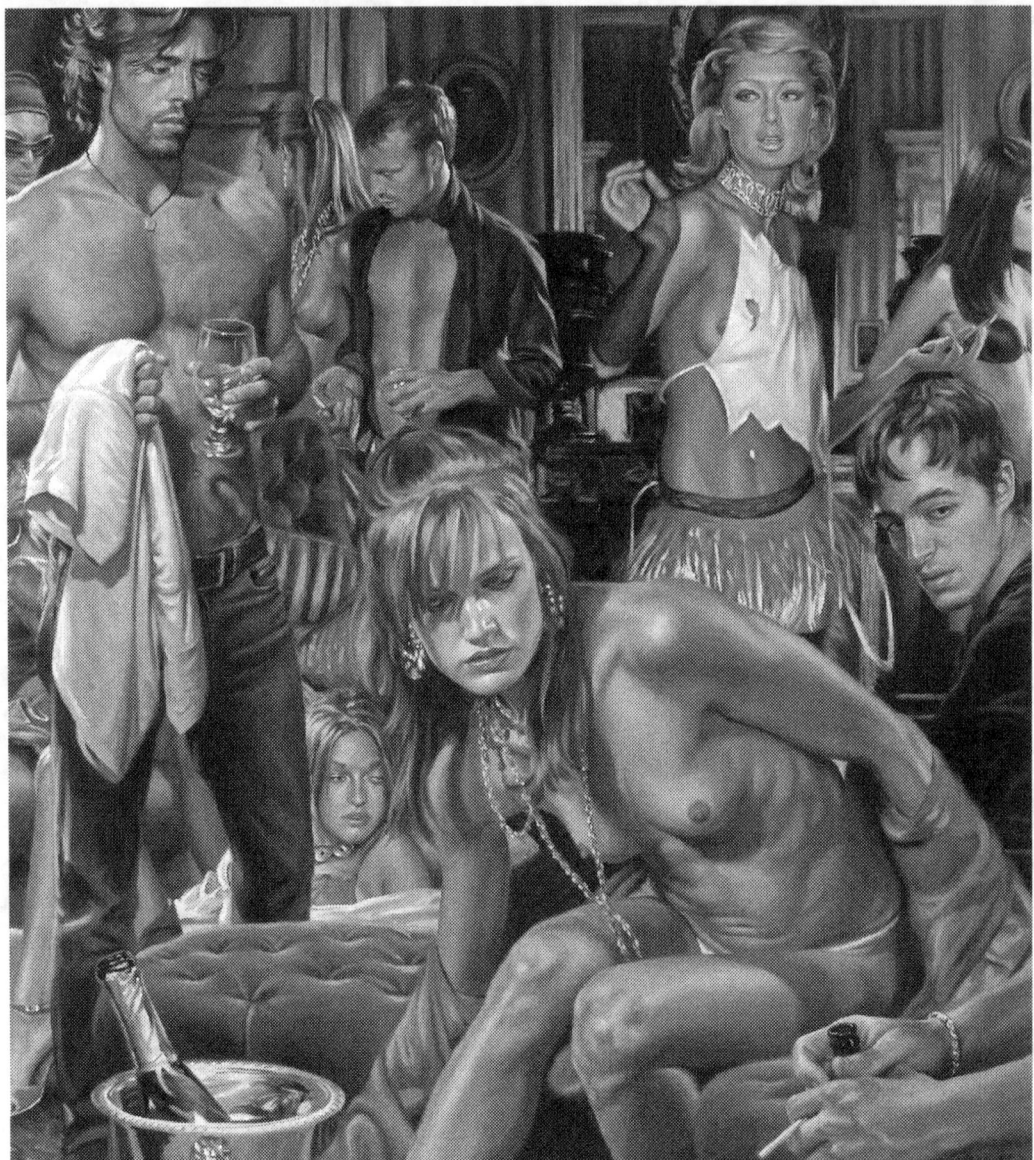

Fig. 17. *Anatomy of Desire* (2004, 66" x 60")

Paris Hilton, famous for being famous, is also desirable for being desirable: rich, young, thin, tall, bold, and apparently unafraid to be herself, though there are not a few social critics who might ask if there is any there there. She hovers in the background like some natural phenomenon—too unnatural to be a person, but too forceful to be a pure construct. Everywhere she goes, she is the center of attention because she is a vacuum, drawing everything toward her by dint of the need to fill the very void she represents and locates. *Anatomy of Desire* was a sensation at the 2004 Armory Show in New York. It could have been sold many times over. Everyone wants what it embodies, which is both the critique of the Paris Hilton non-culture and the culture itself. Everyone sees what they want to see in this painting. Thus desire is anatomized by individual viewers. This defines desire as everything we don't have and even vaguely long for, including the capacity to ignore things we suspect are unworthy of our better selves.

One of Rodgers' favorite models, "Brian," at the left, seems strikingly subdued, almost depressed; what had promised to be an interesting place to be has somehow turned out to be a job he doesn't much like. And the chilled champagne has become nothing more than a prop in the lives of these people. It has to be there to complete their picture of such a scene, but there is no pleasure in it. The riveting observation of Horkheimer and Adorno, "Amusement is the prolongation of work in Late Capitalism," is embodied in this painting. We are conditioned by our reading of history to want to be individuals, to be bold, to be original, to be ambitious, and, above all, to be fulfilled. The ambition *to be* can become a vocation. At some primitive level, sexuality is the most basic form of ambition and being. To want many beautiful bodies is the active fantasy of many young people and the pathetic, lingering dream of a few old ones. At this simplistic level, desire is to have it all. To have them all. And then add in the material things for good measure. Everything is objectified, commidified, present for the shopping and purchasing. We buy others with ourselves, with our time and our effort, and our tattered integrity. Our personality is our marketing machine.

And yet how fragile we are. Cupid's arrow is the fragment of a nearly-lost mythical image that we half-learn as soon as we can think. This apparently innocent fantasy allows us to believe in a powerful but essentially benevolent outside influence, represented by the arrow that pierces the victim. Why not be open to such an outside influence? Unless, of course, it doesn't really come from the outside. Spinoza considered desire the actual essence of being and defined it as conscious appetite. The source and power of desire seems often to be located outside of us, but it feels like it originates from within as well, even if it is a result of a complex convergence of genetics, conditioning, and local or even global circumstance. In spite of an age of terror and trauma, when fear would seem to have the upper hand, desire continues to define us. (What is fear or pain or grief but the source of a hugely powerful desire for something to go away!) The categories of desire may change, but desire itself is a constant, and it is lucrative. The sources and destinations of desire in the culture describe the culture, and the specific desires we have, consciously or not, define each of us, liberating and limiting us in immeasurable ways. We can dedicate ourselves to eliminating desire from our lives, we can willingly, even passionately enslave ourselves, or we can succumb to some semi-conscious, perhaps formally religious compromise.

In fact, Rodgers' work can be seen to explore the paths of desire in world culture of the early twenty-first century. Although he appears to paint exclusively American subjects and settings, he is doing so at a time when things American are inevitably the locus of desire, and when they're not, the locus of anti-desire, of hatred, of the desire to destroy, remove, obliterate, supplant, eradicate. In global commerce, desire takes the familiar form of profit-orientation; in politics, it is incarnated as power; and in the personal zone, it most often manifests itself as that familiar sexual or romantic longing so characteristic of young adults, or that craving for any kind of contact that sadly typifies their elders. In religion, desire is understood in two primary, quite contradictory ways: as an entity in itself that must be avoided, resisted, and escaped from; and as a means and an energy that facilitates a closer approach to God. In many ways, twenty-first century popular culture, especially toward the high end, is indistinguishable from a well-organized, well-established, and fervently-practiced religion.

In a work that achieves something like the scope of a religious fresco, Rodgers' *American Rhapsody* appeared as a wraparound cover for *Flaunt Magazine* (August 2003). The painting is dense, almost overdone, but to a purpose, as if it's an advertising mural for twenty-first century American youth and celebrity culture. This is really a crowd scene, and any of these characters must have desired to be there because it's competitive and uncomfortably close. It's partly a comment about the crowds of beautiful people one encounters everywhere in the up-scale zip codes of the United States, and about how strange the ideal of popular culture is that you have to be rich, young, thin, and beautiful and also be together with other rich, young, thin, and beautiful people. But to what end? They get together and discover that they're still lonely. One is inclined to ask, "Where does their life actually begin?" Everything here seems like backstage preparation: doing make-up, rehearsing lines and gestures, remembering entrances and exits, gaining courage from the other performers who are also getting ready to go on.

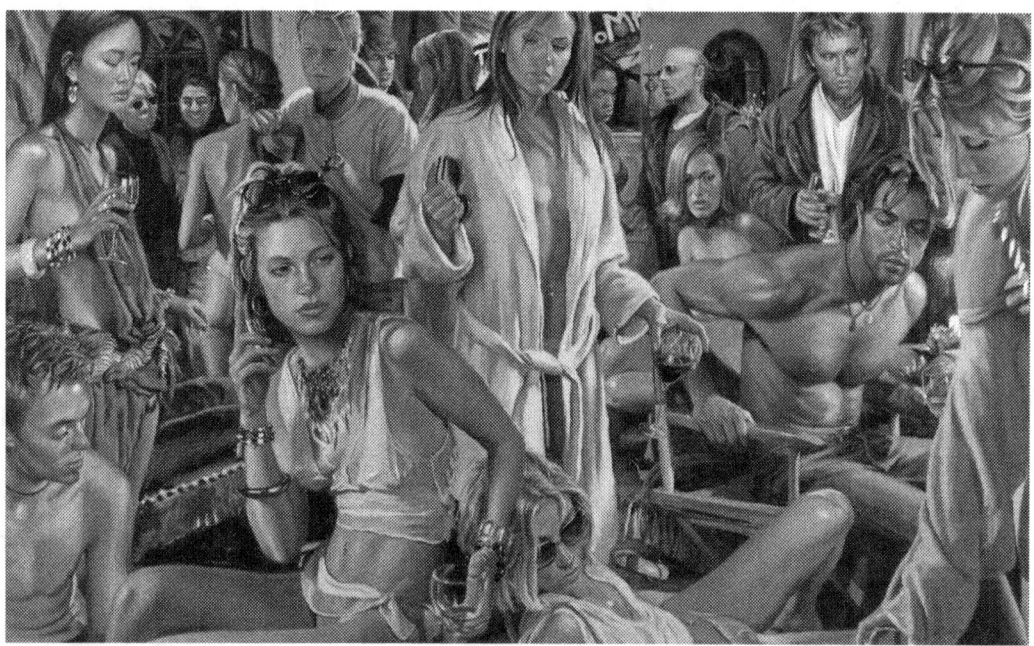

Fig. 18. *American Rhapsody* (2003, 56" x 94")

In the era of a stupendously profitable Hollywood movie that glorifies the suffering of Christ, *American Rhapsody* is a strangely serene version of Jesus and the multitudes. But the Christ figure in the midst of this microcosmic multitude is a woman, and her face is not beatific. She might be thinking about something, perhaps how to keep feeding these people; she shows up like an emblem of pensive grace in the midst of the vulgar throng. Her bare chest is revealing and opens her up to us, but her clothing suggests an ancient style of robe in the midst of the contemporary dress and undress. The structure harks back to religious painting, with its symmetry and apparent symbolism in the right and left sides of the painting. But it's a secular religion, of course, one ornamented with highly-competitively marketed brands and observed through carefully controlled, stylized attitudes and behaviors that are on display in the streets and night clubs. Perhaps the ritualized space of the fashion runway is the closest thing to a sacred place and practice for this religion. This female messianic figure will be sacrificed inevitably (to the needs of the mass culture), as she was crucified on the spine of *Flaunt*. There she is, immortalized in the glossy world, from which she will return and return. It is a mystical painting in its secular banality. In the background is another piece of Schnabel's, that darling of the large-scale New York gallery culture, with his recent gigantic conceptual-cum-realist portraits (and who also happens to make movies).

Rodgers' paintings persistently raise the question about whether we live in relation to people or just in relation to our ideas of people. Our fantasies, constructs, and mistaken perceptions seem to be the truest guides we have. Can we know who we are, much less who anyone else is? Can we know who we are if we cannot know the people we see in front of us? The possibility of living an uncompromised life seems like the greatest fantasy because it is necessary and inevitable that we live a life that is repeatedly and completely compromised, if not absolutely ignorant, blind, and ineffectual. Spiritual projects have historically defined questions and sought answers to the problem of how to see ourselves, how to relate to others, and how to live our lives. As Stephen Cope writes in *Yoga and the Quest for the True Self (301)*, "...in the yogic view, the great problem of life is desire—clinging, craving, greed, holding on"; "...our desire for life to be the way we want it to be, rather than the way it is." Cope speaks of The Upanishads' "idea of sacrifice," which "must be internalized through the inward art of surrendering attachment and desire."

Philosophers continue to analyze the problem in secular terms. Judith Butler, the scholar who has addressed the theoretical bases of desire most exhaustively, beginning with *Subjects of Desire* (1987), points out that Foucault has argued that desire became in the twentieth century "a preoccupation of discourse." In her essay on "Desire" in *Critical Terms for Literary Study* (Lentricchia and McLaughlin, eds.) she asks, "How is it that desire becomes an object of...discourse in general?" Rodgers might answer that it is desire that makes our heart beat, and that we are gradually learning how to talk about it, or represent it, without falling back on simple-minded symbols and language that have to do merely with sex and commerce. Like the invisible air, desire is all around us and will finally be systematized and scientific, and then we will eventually discover a greater, more compelling mystery. But not for centuries, most likely, so we need not worry that we will soon suffer the loss of our favorite mode of mystery.

In her effort to understand contemporary desire, Butler takes us all the way back to Plato to approach desire through allegory: "If allegory is in its most general formulation a way of giving narrative form to something which cannot be directly narrativized, then what does it mean that desire is approached through allegory?" To Rodgers, it just means that desire can only be investigated seriously if we use every available means, and his work verges on allegory in many of his paintings, including *The Labyrinth, Cross Currents, Timepiece, Morea, Halloween Breakfast*, and *This Is Our Youth*. Butler points out that "language is bound to founder on the question of desire" and that it is "forced to seek modes of indirection." Rodgers is a painter of indirection. Or of so many directions that none is immediately obvious, and none dominant.

"Is all desire a desire to return to an impossible origin?" Butler goes on to ask, invoking Plato and Lacan, and echoing Freud. And, "Can the various aims of desire be understood through recourse to a metaphysical trajectory of desire?" Rodgers has independently posed similar questions. Butler speaks of "cultural formations"; Rodgers paints them. The question arises whether desire is "metaphysically conditioned," or whether there are "social arrangements." Rodgers would seem to have it both ways. Butler notes that there are "desires that language brings," including advertising. In manipulating non-verbal signs, Rodgers suggests the ways in which, as Baudrillard has put it, in *Simulacra and Simulation* (87), "All current forms of activity tend toward advertising," and it is interesting to note that other magazines besides *Flaunt* have lately jumped on the Rodgers bandwagon, including *Vegas* (a feature article) and *Elle* (a commissioned painting to accompany an article). Rodgers gets to have it both ways in this regard too, both critiquing and embodying what Baudrillard observes: "Today what we are experiencing is the absorption of all virtual modes of expression into that of advertising. All original cultural forms, all determined languages are absorbed in advertising because it has no depth, it is instantaneous and instantaneously forgotten. Triumph of superficial form, of the smallest common denominator of all signification, degree zero of meaning, triumph of entropy over all possible tropes. The lowest form of energy of the sign." But Rodgers' work on canvas and linen is more than an image that a magazine can use for its own purposes. It is an object and a document in itself; it is its own vector of desire. The project of making large oil paintings that confront this triviality and superficiality of expression and communication is brilliant, bold, and, in various dimensions, revelatory. Finally, however, what remains is great painting—great in size, great in concept, and great in execution.

As Butler has it, "For Plato, to desire is to be moved"; and "desire acquires a body." For Spinoza, "...appetitive desire exists first, and it implies that the soul is moved by what is outside itself, by the external sensuous world." "The human body, that 'earthly form,' only *appears* to be self-moved but is really moved through a reaction to what is not itself." Butler explains that Plato needs "his figure...because the human bodily form only comes into being through being figured in and by its appetitive desire." For Plato, "a body emerges *from* a desire." For Freud, "the bodily ego" involves the notion that "desire is projected and takes a visual form." And, "In Lacan, the body will emerge from the transfiguration of desire into an imaginary visual field, one which establishes the body first as a function of a specular imaginary reflection." Butler notes that "desire might be said to be formative." Plato argues, "There is a certain natural age at which human nature is desirous of procreation," and Rodgers is painting that procreative age in his most recent work, with the obvious irony that these characters are all about consumption, not creation.

Butler writes that "the object of longing or desire" is the "expression and creation of 'the beautiful,'" which is "the character of a certain kind of creation." "Love...is defined in terms of a longing for the beautiful..." that is "only a condition for the possibility of conception and creation," and "conception and generation" is an end in itself—both "natural and creative" and "spiritual and psychic." Rodgers' paintings are "things of the spirit" that emerge from the "domain of ideal forms" but are modified, qualified, accentuated, and heightened by the brilliant details that *mortalize* them. In Diotama's speech in *Symposium*, in which she explains how Love was born of Aphrodite and discusses desire with Socrates, Butler notes this: "…it is the visible that necessarily conditions the insight into the true, even as the true will be distinguished ultimately from both the visible and the 'seeming.'" Rodgers' paintings provide us with "phenomenal conditions" to aid us in understanding our time and place, our cultural present. His paintings make of knowing "a desirous and creative activity."

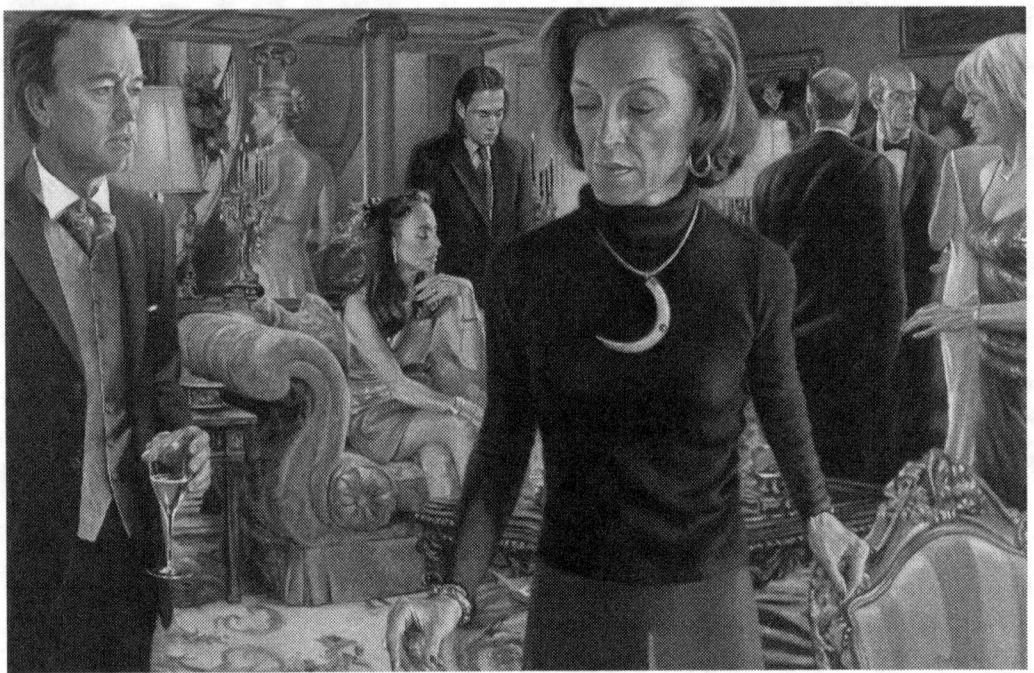

Fig. 19. *A Sleeping Sense of Life According to Love* (2002, 50" x 80")

In *A Sleeping Sense of Life According to Love,* "the vector of the main male character's palpable desire is matched by the necklace the woman wears, resisting the force of his yearning. The combination of her down-turned glance and the curve of the necklace powerfully suggests the vector of her own protective desire. Four other figures in the painting also contribute down-turned heads that seem to form a chorus of unreceptivity: there will be no connection tonight, no fulfilled desire, nothing that easy, nothing of a need so baldly stated being satisfied. This painting is about the delicacy of our tentative internal balance in the face of and in spite of all that we do to create the best of all possible worlds, a refined environment for possibly very unrefined (perhaps repressed) feelings. Our studied, careful posture provides scant permanent protection from the violence, pressures, unbalancing, and instability confronting us, all the forces against us that wear us down, the erosion and relentless friction. The Chaim Soutine painting in the background, *Portrait of a Boy* (also known as *The Servant*), suggests the service that the rest of the world provides people like this, a service that will never be sufficient to awaken the profoundest parts of their sleeping being. Rodgers has, in this painting, represented forms of being in which human experience can get lost. Butler tells us, "...Plato writes that this eternal oneness designated by the domain of forms 'will be neither words nor knowledge'" and that "...we can only know the love of the beautiful through what appears." Rodgers chases down and interrogates our ideas of "beauty" and "cool" as represented in fashion, magazine imagery, motion picture iconography, houses, parties, and conversations. He presents what is beyond the word, a "standing outside oneself" or "ek-stasis." By contemplating these figures who are in some sense "beside themselves," we can (if we choose to) meditate on our own place, person, and integrity, as it relates to both physical and psychological conditions. The complications and confusions of our desires can paralyze us, but, if examined with utter sincerity and humility, they can show us our way when we think we have lost it.

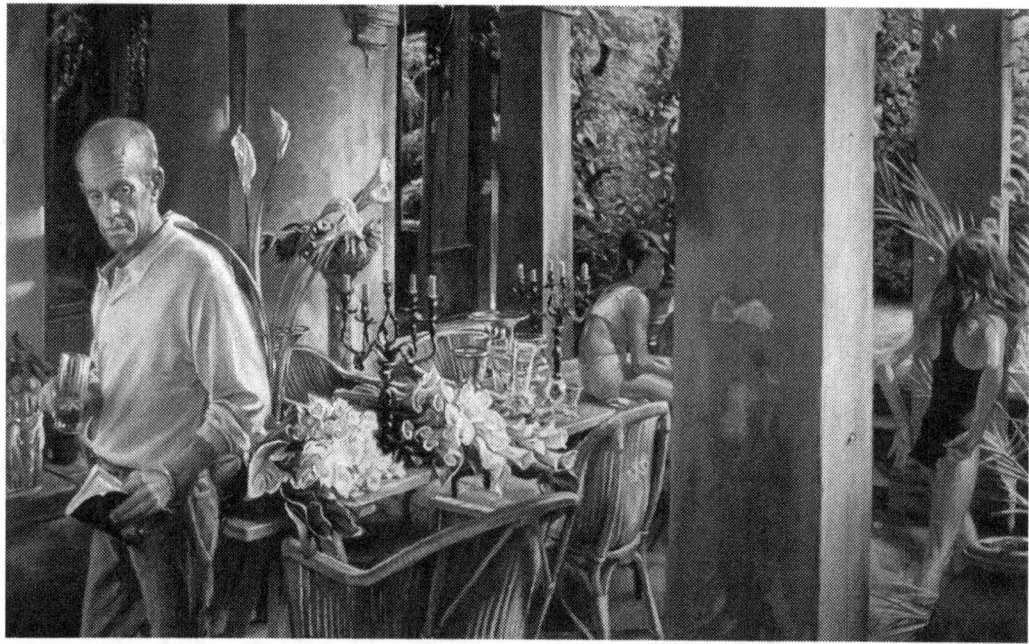

Fig. 20. *And Then There Were None* (1999, 48" x 81")

In one of the more foreboding pictures Rodgers has made, *And Then There Were None,* a magnificent painting in subdued tones, the middle-aged male figure at the far left dominates the scene, even from the edge of the painting, where he seems to have lost his way entirely. His head and face are memorable, even haunting, and his backward-tending glance generates a hint of menace, even as the way he holds a book, fingers marking his place, suggests a civilized, humane soul, who would mean no harm to the innocents who play nearby. Unless he couldn't help himself. The flower-bedecked table divides the adult from the children's world, but the children themselves are rendered more vulnerable by the pillar between them. There is a suggestion of some coming festivity in the flowers, the children's buoyancy, and their youthful motion, which is in exact opposition to the man who shows all of his cares in his face and forehead, a locus of tentativeness and brooding reflection. There is something he's very conscious of, perhaps the lack of that thing that the energy and optimism of childhood remind him was his once and now is forever lost. His empty glass, open book, and the cornucopia of stuff spilling toward him, the bounty of which is not available to him emotionally, all indicate emotional spaces and moments that have passed him by. The Stonehenge-like columns, huge primitive standing columns, are in a jungle-like setting; they seem to stand for immutable complexity that doesn't daunt the running kid but has stumped, stopped, or crushed this man. The Garden of Eden motif runs riot, creating an exaggeration or even a caricature of innocence and plenty. The little girl's gesture with the bathing suit adjustment is the final punctuation: his life is comparatively over, behind him, uninteresting to her. Life is beginning all over again, and it is leaving him behind, or, even more eerily, forcing him to flee toward his death. So much seems available in this young world, and yet everything he most cares about is inaccessible. There once seemed to be many people, possibilities, and desires for him, and now there are none. In *Quiet Days in Clichy,* Henry Miller remarks, "For an artist, bad situations are just as fertile as good ones, sometimes even more so." For the painter, in this case, the painting emerges from his imagination of a character's disastrous, doomed life. But Miller, ever the optimist, even as he plumbs the depths of degradation and despair, also observes, "Life is constantly providing us with new funds, new resources, even when we are reduced to immobility." For the man in *And Then There Were None,* who might remind us of a slightly twisted Henry Miller, this seems a little too optimistic.

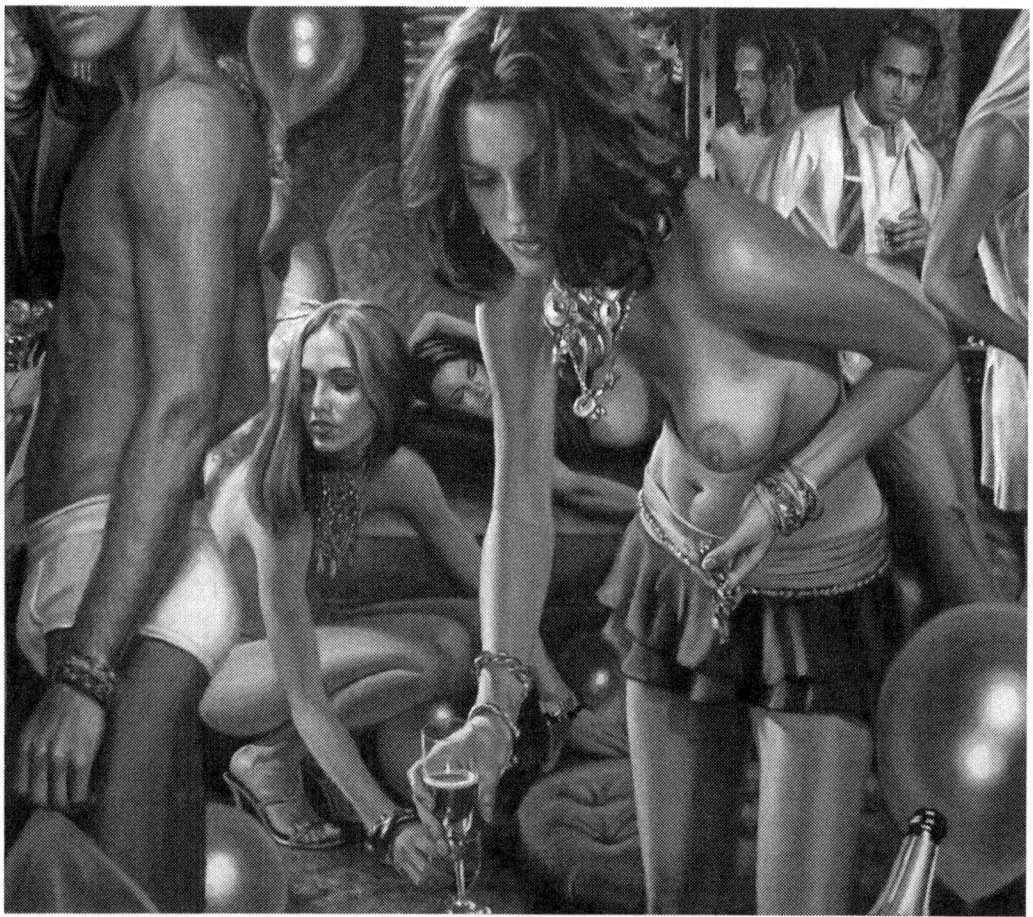

Fig. 21. *Approximations of Immortality* (2003, 48" x 56")

But gloom and doom is not what Rodgers is about, at root. He is playful in everything he undertakes, both in relation to content and technique, and in *Approximations of Immortality* Rodgers plays with the idea of the fantasy of eternal, youthful life via the distortions of "realism," by tweaking the color to make everything seem strangely unreal. This is a dark painting, all about their bodies and what they're up to, not about moments of interiority. It is an accurate rendition of a cultural moment: place, space, styles, differences in physical reality (the skinny girl on the left with the sharp face, the girl with the little "pooch" to her tummy, that oh-so-mortal female looseness of the belly hanging, and the pendulous breasts, not exactly conforming to the stylized ideal, the suave dude in the white shirt, and the guy with weird hair behind him—people of all kinds who squeezed into this party). The young face of the woman in front contrasts with the worldly face of the guy behind. Here is the commercialization of our lives—dressed and undressed. She wears her pendulous breasts like her dependent necklace. There is more sexual innuendo here than in most of the other paintings, and not just from her body. This is more like people on the prowl, especially the guy with the tie. He seems to be paying attention to her and not paying attention to a thought he is having on his own: looking at her for her. She seems almost to be aware of him, unlike the central female figure in *All About Eve*, who was turned inward. In this case, it's more like she's up to something. The squatting woman doesn't seem to have much interior consciousness either. Hers has the look of a face being looked at, blank and on display. But, in the case of the central figure, the brunette's facial expression smacks of being surreptitious (and repetitious in the context). She lets her arm and mouth hang, holds the champagne, and seems to be hiding something. She is, in effect, hidden under her hair and behind her breasts. She is shielding her thoughts, maybe even from herself. Hans Furth, in *Knowledge As Desire*, states, "As with Freud's morality, when knowledge tries to hide its libidinous origin, it is cut off from its constructive energy and is left to operate in a restrictive and ultimately destructive manner. Far from being opposed to each other, human emotions and knowledge, desire and object, are two sides of the same coin and have their common origin in the biological evolution of human sociability and in the individual development of each child" (172). Rodgers shows very young people—very recently children—and how these helpless creatures try to both chase after and avoid their animal selves. And he portrays older people, both in their presence and in their absence, who try to convince themselves that they are superior to the beasts of the earth.

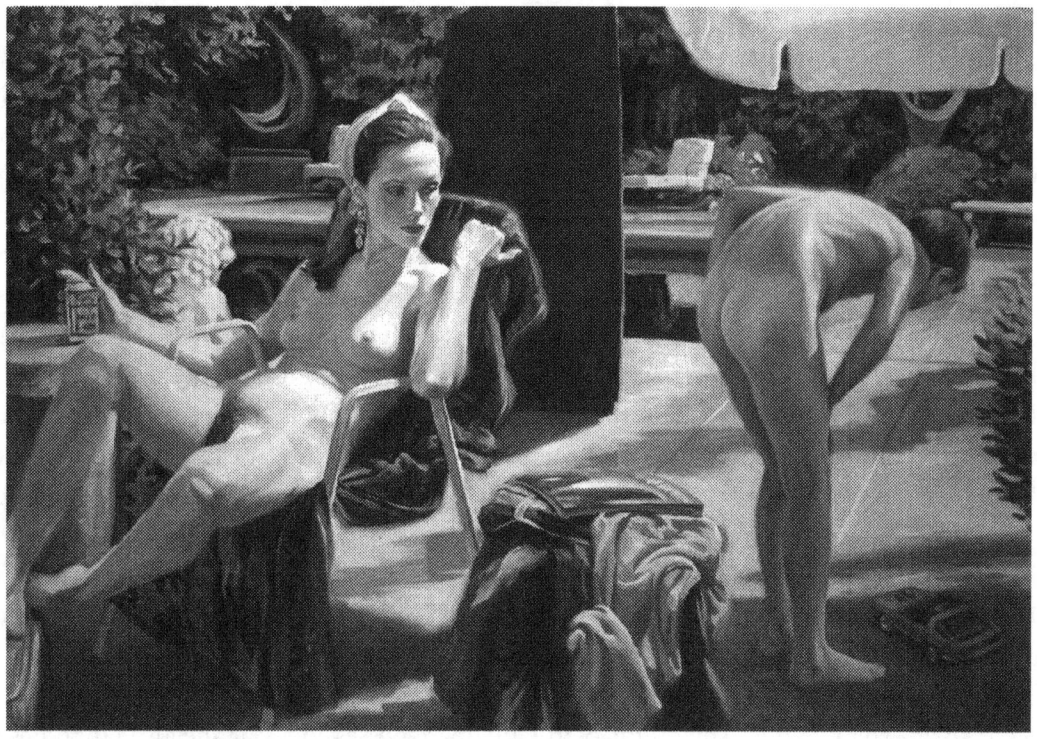

Fig. 22. *His Collection* (1994, 54" x 80")

Our essential animal essence is one of Rodgers' favorite themes, and so many of his characters are hunting, or hunted, or alert to something in the wind. *His Collection* is a dazzling, even breathtaking private scene that features a central female character who has the air of a zoo creature. Like *Halloween Breakfast*, this picture suggests both genre painting and narrative. It is a very personal, domestic, somewhat exclusive scene, but an obviously unremarkable circumstance to the participants although, to us, alarms are going off immediately. The blinding light of the woman's nakedness is like the visual equivalent of a siren going off. In the realm of pure domestic normality and banality, we can accept this as a kind of *fin de siecle* American corruption that is in itself harmless, and yet we get the suggestion of all sorts of illicit and subterranean interests. Presumably, there is a relationship between the unseen husband and father and this woman, who, because of her posture and the viewer's privileged position as voyeur, seems like someone altogether available in a sinister sense, and who is also weirdly interested in this seemingly quite innocent boy's bottom. Or is it only the viewer who makes that connection?

The viewer who has seen Fischl's famous "bad boy" painting certainly makes some kind of connection. It's not clear that there is any prurient interest on her part but because of her gesture and posture, you wonder what her life is, and what her thoughts are. She's clearly in a private space, mentally and physically. It's a private pool that serves as a stage for very exclusive private lives, as well as the venue for an impressive but not significant art collection. The woman is one more piece of collected sculpture, like the three large pieces: the bronze on the left, like a confused slice of moon; the cast concrete on right; the large simple form of green steel behind the woman; and the almost comical cast-stone lion off to the left—all of it what Rodgers calls "show-off stuff." The presence of the car represents the larger world of which the probable husband and father is a part. Everybody seems to have playthings, all of which imitate high-end ideas. The absent man plays with fancy sculpture and women, the child plays with symbols of the world he will inherit, and the woman probably plays with the pile of magazines and clothes at the very center of the painting. It's all so banal. An older "he" is clearly implied. Faced with the plain lush magnificence of her alabaster torso and hips, we are aware that something magical is hinted at, but it's not clear what it is or how it gets there. The brilliant light on her skin is a shimmering revelation, but of what? The extravagant nudity is suggestive of something, not to mention the apparent ease and comfort and pleasure of it. It's as if everything's going off in other directions, but she hints of something magical—beyond sexual—in the painting, more interesting than any of the sculpture that he owns. As a "trophy wife," she might be the ultimate possession, but she also embodies something beyond possession, something that one can imagine her husband is fascinated by because she is both "his" and also an entity, a being, so far beyond his grasp.

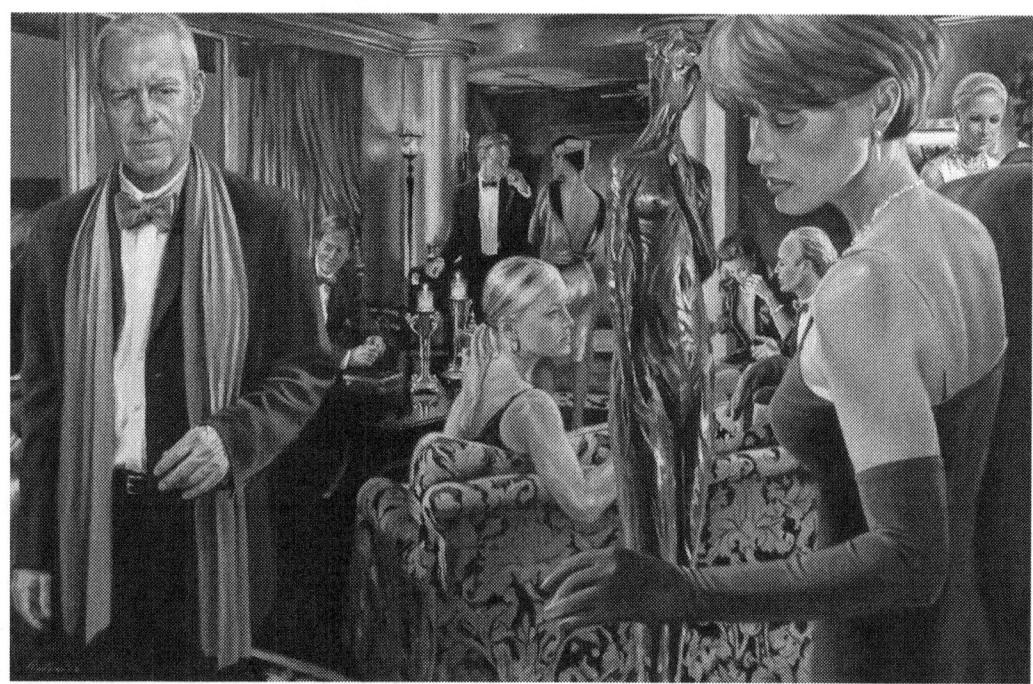

Fig. 23. *Apollonian Rhythms* (2002, 48" x 76 ½")

Andy Grundberg, in an essay on David Levinthal's photography, writes, "The human body is of pressing interest today because of two polar impulses: repression and desire." *Apollonian Rhythms* explores the carefully orchestrated camouflage and sublimation of desire, if not its absolute repression. The major vectors are united in turning away from the central sculpture, whose abstracted erotic quality drives them to cover themselves according to their own formal habits of social protection. Three things stand out in this picture, first, the hidden but overt sexuality that the women display, the two near women with the bare shoulders, semi-proffered chests, and long bare suggestive backs, their prominent but disguised flesh. The Zorro-like arm masked in long glove is an exaggerated presence. Next, there is the central sculpture of the naked form, completely stylized if not abstracted. It creates a play back and forth between the breast on the sculpture and the breast in the black dress pointing at each other, one disguised in a strange, abstracted quality, bronzed and decorative, and the other coyly prominent and yet hidden in the context of the body's public posture. Then, there is the frank look of the man on the left; his expression shows up in relation to the camouflaged and subdued sexuality of everything and everyone around him. He is handsome but not attending to or flaunting or hiding his possible sexual potency. The women's sexuality is embodied in high style: hair, make-up, clothes. The space is outfitted in a similar high style: semi-gaudy and semi-stylish couch, curtains. There is also a complex architecture to the painting, including arms, faces, gestures, couches, poles, ceilings, light. It is a rhythmic, constructed, stilted, over-decorated space. It's all very idealized within which their sexuality finds itself as almost an unnatural player. The man's face and head remains something apart, both concerned and peaceful. The characters' behavior and dress mirrors their environment, but they don't seem to respond to it or have an affinity for it—it's not a mirror of their inside. They live in a constrained propriety. The closest thing to an escape from all of this is the stiff, controlled sculpture.

In the case of the woman in the right foreground, there is the slight plumpness of the top of the arm, cheek, and lips, and more and more you can see so much going on with her. The room is evidently meant to be a rich interior but shows up as a phony place, and yet the people have an unreleased, authentic vitality. All of this complexity buzzes against that weird plane of blue sky in the left background, indicating the unknowable universe outside their very modern construct, which is their own created interior, their limited and poignantly human notion of beauty. We can almost feel the back-and-forth dynamic between blue emptiness and plainness and the overwrought and overdone couch, not to mention the architecture. There is really no room for humanity, and yet there is that man existing beatifically and very much in it, and the redhead increasingly revealed in her vulnerability that is not part of this false world, but is in fact uncontrollably human and vulnerable. Everything else is controlled, ordered. What we call sexual and what we call stylistic echoes each other—as if they order their sexuality the way they order their apartment. One wonders what goes on when merely one person is "at home" in that space, comfortably and casually. But, here, now, in this scene, the women are disporting themselves in a different way: they design their personal affects just as they choose their personal effects—and they even design the effects they have on others. Everything is by design. The women wear sexually suggestive clothing—it's in the culture—whereas the men are constrained. To be sexual, the idea of a man with a shoulder-baring garment is ludicrous. All of this puts a lot of pressure on the women, who have to reveal so much more than hands and faces. And aging becomes the men under these conditions because "rugged" on men is desirable.

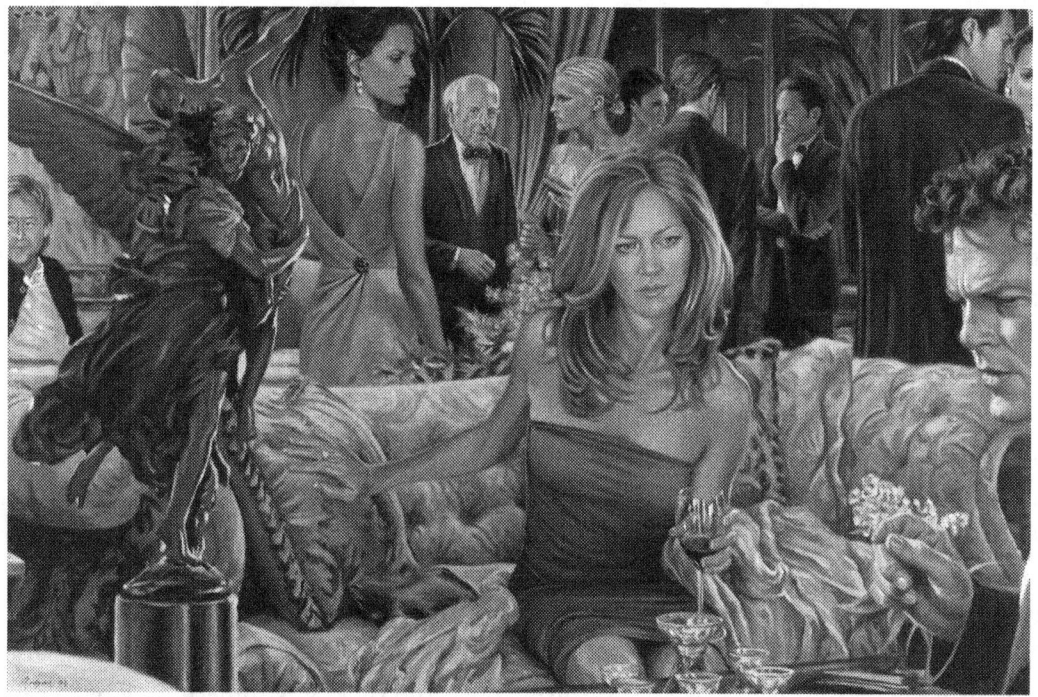

Fig. 24. *Between Two Worlds* (2002, 54" x 83")

Similarly, *Between Two Worlds* investigates constructed and repressed desire. This painting includes the self-portrait of the artist leaning into his own picture—or perhaps getting ready to leave the picture, alive to a new idea for another picture. Rodgers' self-portrait here recalls the older male in *Apollonian Rhythms*, but the male figure here is more dynamic, less caught in between. The whole arrangement is a carefully constructed image that is built upon vectoral conflict that sends our eyes back and forth, in and out, up and down, and diagonally across the expanse of the canvas. The central female character works almost as a pop-art super-woman. She is thinly-painted, and her "beauty" is almost caricatured. The realism of Rodgers' art here bursts out of its thin skin and cries conception, abstraction, creation, even cartoon. The painting is on the verge of becoming a comic-book illustration of a Socratic dialogue about beauty, truth, wisdom, age, youth, art, and meaning.

Fay Gold, the owner of Fay Gold Galleries in Atlanta, and one of the "wise women" in Joyce Tenneson's book of the same name (*Wise Women: A Celebration of Their Insights, Courage, and Beauty,* 2002), was one of the early champions of Rodgers' work. She points to the "perfection" of his paintings as a way of representing desire in which there are no flaws in the bodies he presents for our inspection, unlike the figures in Botero's and Pearlstein's work. "Terry's are all perfect," she marvels. "It's a perfect package. But every one of them looks troubled. No one is making eye contact. They're all caught up in their own particular world at that moment. Now that makes them live." Gold has shown many of Rodgers' works, sold many, and discussed the paintings with hundreds of art lovers who have attended the shows. "The fact that the people in the paintings are not making eye contact makes us wonder what the problem is, what's wrong. What are they thinking? Where are they going? Something's always about to happen to each of them. And we don't know exactly what's going to happen next."

Gold believes the conditions of the paintings tend toward the allegorical, precisely because we do not know what will happen next: "…it puts them into the category of allegory. It leaves reality, totally, and goes into a surreal situation…[because]…it's not possible that everyone is caught up in their own ego and their own existence to not make eye contact. Everyone who sees the paintings notices that. But they don't reject it because they've been there themselves." Gold is impressed by the boundaries she sees between character and character, and between each character and their surroundings. "They are all separate; the more the rooms get crowded, the more isolated each character becomes. Terry is able to isolate them somehow."

Gold sees a progression in Rodgers' work. "It started with people having a kind of paranoia. In the earlier paintings, people were very suspicious. And there was something a little bit evil…with the children, or someone possibly hurting the children, or having some secret agenda. Even though the aspect of secrecy remains, the agenda has become much more social, and much more acceptable, and fun. As the paintings got into the cocktail party stage, there was this proliferation of older men and younger women, and men were pretty much dandies, and the setting was always very affluent. The third stage is this whole concept of fashion, Hollywood. Some other career that Terry might have wanted—as a famous movie star, since he's so handsome himself. I think he may be reliving a scene that he thought he might have missed by not going to Hollywood."

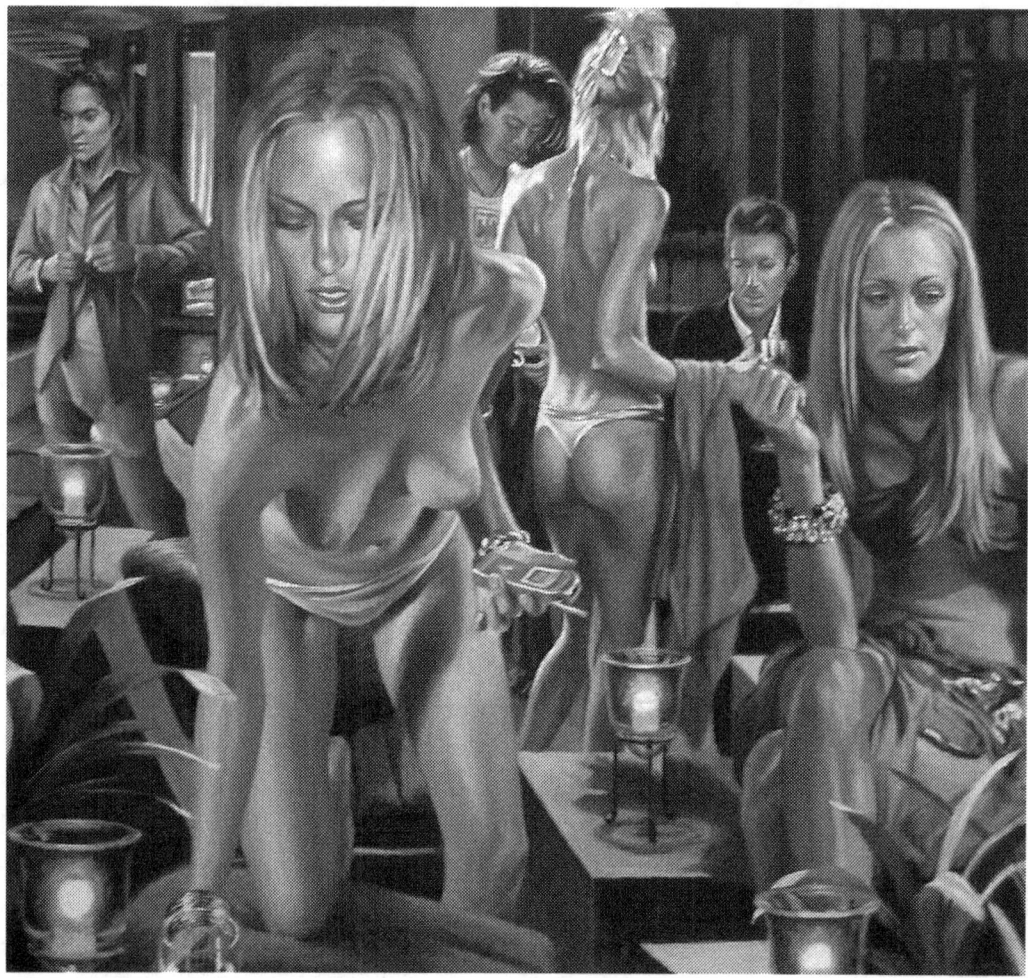

Fig. 25. *The Night Deck* (2003, 48" x 52 ½")

On the streets of New York, Los Angeles, Miami, Milan, or Paris, Rodgers is in fact a dashing figure, his long, curly hair flying behind him as he chases down a possible model, his camera bags bouncing as he runs. The interaction of the photographer-painter and the models he finds is a kind of microcosmic sample of the culture he paints. With amazing frequency, the people he picks out on the streets of New York and Milan turn out to be working professional models. What he makes of all these models and their symbolic role in the broader culture can be seen in *The Night Deck,* in which the central figure comes into our world with her breasts and telephone, reaching for a drink. She has lipstick on but no top. Here are those interesting hues we've seen in *Approximations of*

Immortality and *Geometries of Innocence*. There are four candles. It's just another night and just another party. The guy on the left is getting dressed, and it seems like an odd place to be getting dressed. It emphasizes the in-between quality of the space: are we inside or outside? Is it a private home? Near the ocean or in the city, and if it's the latter, is it Miami or LA? Perhaps he's been in a hot tub. Apparently, it's not abnormal to him or anyone else there, all of them so completely engaged with where their own head is. The only person looking directly is the seated guy, but he's still looking down. They're all self-contained cruise ships passing in the night.

Caught in (Between) the Act(s)

Rodgers is nothing as a painter if not a painter with vision. Everything he does depends on a way of seeing humanity, individuals, the contemporary culture, and the processes by which meaning is so fleetingly manufactured. His mastery of the telling detail (like Degas' *trait saillant*) shows up in every painting, and the key detail may not in fact be a recognizable one. For example, the brushstrokes of the blouse of the middle figure in *The Opacity of Light* contribute to the swirl of the vectors. The bottom of the bathing suit of the woman on the right just shows through. The way the man's shirt sits accentuates the ridges and ripples so that there are more vectors of his twist and turn—again, as often in Rodgers, suggesting the drapery of the Renaissance. The title of this painting recalls something else from Judith Butler, that desire "guarantees a certain opacity in language, an opacity that language can enact and display, but without which it cannot operate." This suggests a whole catalogue of punning truisms, that we cannot really see what we mean, but that we can still mean what we see and say. Rodgers' flood of light accentuates the blindness of the characters, just as our deluge of "communication" these days highlights our time-honored failure to communicate. We seem to assume that, as we grow older and more mature, we will become more adept at connecting with each other. That is why, in addition to the serene beauty of the outdoor scene, *The Opacity of Light* seems to be one of the saddest pictures Rodgers has made.

The effects of showing young adults in difficulty is different. Hope remains possible, no matter how misguided that hope may be. *In Shades of Olympus* and *This Is Our Youth* especially, but in a majority of Rodgers' recent paintings, the focus on the youth culture—not adolescents, but perhaps young adult professionals—is harsh but not condemnatory. Robert Henri asked the question, "Can't we ever realize that it is not for the old to judge the young—that it is the young who must judge the old?" Rodgers seems to allow the generation coming into adulthood to have its moment of possibility in these two paintings, and this applies to *Cartesian Coordinates* and *The Labyrinth*, as well. The generalized desire may be inchoate and even timid, but it seems to exude possibility. Desire can be a mood, a condition, a mode, a climate, or a way of life. More often than not, "desire" is taken to be a synonym for sexual yearning. Men can have a knee-jerk kind of desire because of being genetically "wired to fire," as one wag recently put it. Or it can be known in the context of a "desire for" some very specific non-sexual state or concrete thing: an object, a pre-packaged experience, money, power, status, connections, fame, or simply laying eyes on the face of a loved one. Not to mention the desire for desire. Of course, given that everything in twenty-first century urban American culture is sexualized, desire is most often seen as a titillating experience, possibly verging on the taboo. In fact, it's cool to be right at the edge, pushing the envelope, almost a little over the top. Dangerous. This sustained, heightened state of sensory and emotional alertness is a convenient and commercially effective way of masking the central concern of advanced civilization: what to do with the typically obsessive human energy that is unleashed when there is prosperity, abundance, and leisure—unlimited opportunity and choice—and when meaning and significance are called into question by an advanced education and an intellectual skepticism that can withstand almost anything but the idea of desire itself. Despite the obviousness and pervasiveness of crassly solicitous and even pandering advertisement and promotion that feature desire as the dominant motif, it is still quite common to meet people who seem unconscious of many of the desires they can be observed to be acting on, if not actually organizing their lives around. Shopping is perhaps the prime example. Drinking is another leading motivator. To get high and stay high is the apparent desire of many people who would not actually admit as much. To not be alone is another unconscious desire that seems to be a leading *raison d'etre*. "Anything but solitude without media" could well be the motto of the representative American.

A typical middle- or upper-middle-class response to a representative Rodgers painting is repugnance in an understated, highly controlled way. People will look and then move on, shrinking from trying to see themselves in the canvas. Or perhaps they will linger to speculate on where such a party might actually happen, as if Rodgers is documenting actual parties in actual places with actual people. The naïve will ask, "Where and when did this party happen, and why are people naked?" But if one looks at the brushstrokes, one understands the people, the party, and Rodgers' vision. The brushstrokes tell the story that cannot be apprehended by someone who merely reads the painting for a clue to relationships and chronologies of "real people." The brushstrokes narrate a chaotic American history compressed into a furiously intense present.

I reflect and write about Rodgers' work near a print of Paul Cezanne's 1893 *Ginger Pot with Pomegranate and Pears*. I ask myself about the many odd angles, why everything isn't fully rendered, and why there is such a large blank spot in the upper left. In short, I ask myself what's going on in this painting about a pomegranate and some pears. Of course, what's going on is paint, line, shape, color. And because Cezanne is long-gone, and because these are pears and not people, no one is disturbed by Cezanne anymore—except artists who still feel the urgency and revolutionary energy of his accomplishment. Rodgers makes us feel uneasy in front of the "still lives" he presents, as much because of the painterly brushstrokes as because of the postures, relations, and *dishabille* of his figures.

Possibly the most prominent evidence of desire in sophisticated urban cultures is what Rodgers, echoing Freud, has referred to as "dislocated" or "displaced" desire. It involves a re-direction of natural desires into complicated and wonderfully artificial targets. For example, American consumers are conditioned to be always wanting, seeking, and finding; and American athletes are trained to feel "desire" and to act on it in such a way as to sacrifice everything for the glory attached to incremental acts of controlled rage that are thought to contribute to the collective good of the team, which is to say, to "winning."

The many faces, forces, characteristics, and effects of desire include intoxication, paralysis, inspiration, exhaustion, discovery, and disorientation. Desire can be a wild ride or a perpetual waiting. It can energize and debilitate. It can organize a life or destroy one. It is possible to plot various forms of desire on various axes. Various physical and mental and emotional states could be catalogued. These spectra could show us combinations of desire that might be interesting. A systematic study of the different degrees and kinds of desire might result in ennui versus titillation, for example. A long-term, dedicated desire can be reassuring, can grow on us and root itself in every corner of our existence, but sometimes even a desire to which we are deeply committed can be lost in the maelstrom of mutations generated by the machinery of merchandising and propaganda that is the contemporary media monster. One can lose sight of the big picture; one becomes enmeshed in a thousand details, deadlines, offers, and urgencies. Desire is reduced to window-shopping and web- and TV-surfing. Desire can be fragmented into multiple specific desires, each of which is perishable because of its triviality and extremely short-term character. To be with X, to go to Y, to call Z. Desire can be exhausting. If one pursues one's desire too vigorously, one can even injure oneself.

Baudrillard, in pointing to the "hegemony of the system," observes that we could "exalt the ruses of desire" as a kind of struggle, but Rodgers indicates the many ways in which these "ruses" are in fact part of the hegemonic system and therefore a distraction from the possible purity of a passionately-understood and fully-committed foundational desire. His own desire seems as pure as they come: he loves life, he loves people, he loves to shoot photographs, compose arrangements, and, above all, he loves to paint. In his studio, he keeps the Fairbrother Sargent book open on a chair nearby. A slow freight train vibrates the building as it crosses the viaduct at eye level, but

Rodgers only hears the opera recording blaring from his speakers. He is a bundle of energy, full of desire and showering vectors of energy everywhere he goes—but pouring most of them into the canvas before him. Jackson Pollack designed and performed in a dance of desire, and Gerhard Richter has made a career out of a specific desire—to see how we see ourselves seeing. Rodgers has the physical exuberance of Pollock but not the dead-end self-destructiveness. He admires and uses the techniques of abstract expressionism just as he observes every kind of technique, style, and subject. Like Richter, Rodgers revels in the conceptual aspects of painting and photography, and in exploring their incremental differences.

Rodgers' work traces the paths of a nonverbal rhetoric. He captures the images that are at the heart of cultural propaganda. What was once the province only of philosophers and politicians in verbal contexts is now available to everyone; we are all spinning our own worlds, arguing and persuading and promoting and publicly relating. "I am either painting or watching people," Rodgers says. "I love to look for people and settings that would be a pleasure to paint. This is the greatest time to be alive. Everything has developed to the point at which there are large numbers of people with the opportunity to make sense of their lives, and yet we're not really advanced enough to know how to do it, so there are all of these prosperous and intelligent people struggling with unprecedented choices. I catch them in the act of choosing. Or perhaps in the midst of their indecision and unknowing. In full-blown dilemma, as it were. In that state, they take on a gorgeously innocent quality. They become almost inanimate in a beautiful human way."

He paints people like Cezanne painted mountains and fruit. People as big and significant and pure as mountains, as small and insignificant and pure as apples. As massive and solid and fragile as life. They are presented in mysteriously interesting arrangements, which he manipulates with the same enthusiasm and patience that Cezanne famously manipulated his apples and pears. And every figure and object is rendered so that it exists in and of itself perfectly, and they can be resided with, considered, contemplated, and enjoyed. The wisp of hair over a forehead, the splash of purple that turns out to be a napkin in context has a similar effect to the odd detail in Cezannne's still lifes. Rodgers is brilliant with the "smallest constituent element," as Rilke said of Cezanne, with "the cell" of art. And when all the cells add up, Rodgers has given us "still lives" like snapshots that grow and develop in our consciousness as we try and fail to comprehend what's there.

The inward gaze of Rodgers' subjects indicates that the vectors of their attention appear to be directed at memory, fantasy, or self-evaluation. Their self-monitoring mechanisms seem to render them blind to their surroundings, oblivious to the opulence, decadence, stimulation, and even danger of their immediate environment. They calculate their next move, but not their next actual physical movement, as if they're plotting the next step in a life story, weighing the risk-reward ratio, attempting to decide whether or not to change everything. We see all of this through Rodgers' agency because he documents what Baudrillard calls our "involuntary transperancy." The mental illness commonly called depression may be the greatest threat to healthy Americans. When depression develops, one of the first symptoms is the vague nostalgia for desire: the wish for desire, the desire for desire. James Salter's *A Sport and a Pastime* ends in elegiac melancholy: "They visit friends, talk, go home in the evening, deep in the life we all agree is so greatly to be desired." Baudrillard's take is that "we are all melancholic." "The masses themselves are caught up in a gigantic process of inertia through acceleration." The collective vectors, numberless and potent as they are, cancel each other out.

Desire can be innocently involved with shiny things, new things, rare things. Ugliness and beauty become intermingled. Everything is reduced and simplified to a matter of color and line and light and shadow and shape. To see is everything. Later, there will be time for thinking. We know that, as Heidegger put it, "We come too late for the Gods and too soon for being." Rodgers is a student of human behavior, the human form, and the human struggle for authenticity in an age when most scientists and intellectuals agree that the only road signs we have to rely on are ancient, incomplete, or as yet undiscovered. He watches people, he asks them to pose, discovers them as if they are the only people on earth. His studio houses thousands of photographs, many of them in casual piles. His office at home has more. The constants in his daily professional life are shooting photos and making paintings, while the people in Rodgers' painted world seem to experience the flux of Heraclitus as their only constant. "This shaking keeps me steady," Roethke wrote.

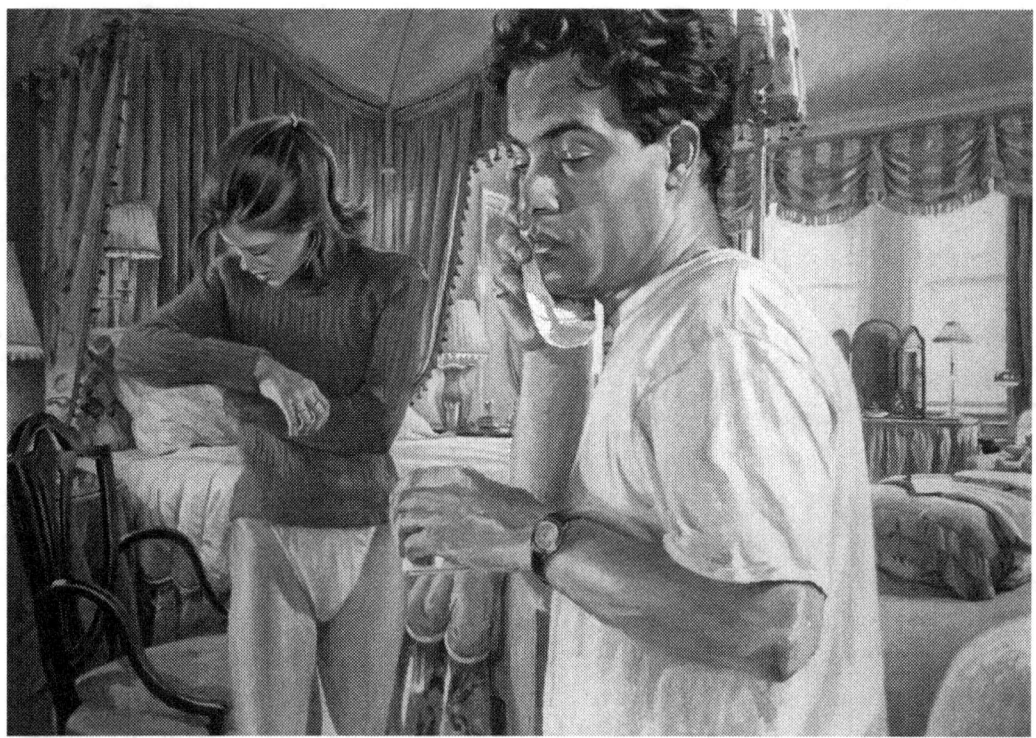

Fig. 26. *The Conversation* (2000, 48" x 70")

Rodgers loves people: the way they look, the way they talk, the way they dress, and the way they interact (or don't). His work invites us to ask what other people are to us. Hell, as Sartre said, or something else? The Holy Grail? Are other people destinations, vehicles, distractions, or even, for those of us who love scapegoats, our doom? Some gurus and saints might suggest that we don't need other people, that we're better off without them. That we need nothing when we desire only peace. But the fact of life for many people is that the sweet peace of solitude rapidly decays into an aching loneliness. What kind of company do we desire? We all crave the best kind of intimate company, and yet it often goes awry, as in *The Conversation*. Here is another painting done in a decorative palette with sinister content. The title suggests communication, but the image suggests the lack of it. Active avoidance of it. The oh-so-subtle uncertainty of it all, the uncertain relationship (could it even be father and daughter?), the slightly opulent bedroom, unless of course they're just visiting, or staying in some kind of hotel or up-scale bed and breakfast. There is the possibility that she's leaving and he doesn't care. The homey ultra-decorated environment is where everybody in America supposedly would like to live, or at least have the opportunity to despise.

"Bad taste," one might say, "I wouldn't have that" (even if I could). The incident that we're watching is indeterminate, as are so many of the incidents and non-incidents Rodgers paints in a way that suggests narrative but stops short of indicating it. Is the significant conversation the one that he's having on the phone (as he ignores her), or is it between the two of them, and has been interrupted? The suggestions of something significant going on seem both evident and unclear. Like *Private Domain*, this painting's situation seems to owe something to Degas' enigmatic *Interior*.

Private Domain captures the riddle of desire as it relates to notions of sex and freedom, how desire is both central and marginalized, creative and sustaining on the one hand, and, on the other, destructive. Desire inserts itself in our lives in ways that sometimes stop just short of verifiable behaviors. In this case, the woman, looking conventionally desirable, ignores the man behind her in favor of the laptop computer on the bed in front of her, where, presumably she engages in something more desirable than interaction with him. She escapes her material surroundings in order to exist in a place that is more (or less) than her own private fantasy. She might be vitally engaged in something in her own mind, but she is in some important sense absent from "the here and now."

Here and now is where we are better off, but the yawning chasms of past and future beckon and threaten on opposite sides, and we are perilously balanced in between. The idea that an ideal person (not the one we're stuck with) could save us from ourselves and our various dilemmas is suggested in many of Rodgers' works. I would be fine if I just had X: validated, authenticated, and fulfilled (or at least sedated). "The Unanimous Declaration of the Thirteen United States of America," is familiarly known the world over as "The Declaration of Independence," and now almost universally, though semi-consciously, regarded as a kind of private, personal birthright. In a little book in my possession that includes this famous document, there is a glossary that features neither "pursuit" nor "happiness," the vector and the destination that Jefferson suggested all Americans—and, by extension, all human beings—have a right to. Desire is now seemingly more than a right; it is mandatory. It is not temptation or inclination or simple hankering, but a kind of moral requirement. Spending, seeking, striving, and competing are practiced daily as a religious ritual, but how shall we find the desire that will make all of this activity meaningful? At this writing, *The Wall Street Journal* (June 15, 2004) reports that 18-year-old Allegra Versace has inherited half of the famous fashion empire. She won't have any role in running the company; it's reminiscent of a child king or queen with a regent. And what does she want to take up? "Acting," because that way she can "be a different person every day." Other than an apparent ignorance of an actor's actual life experience, this is both pathetic and poignant because of its prescience; she already knows that she won't be able to bear being only herself. The ultimate desire today for the young woman who can have anything she wishes is not to be who she is for more than one day at a time.

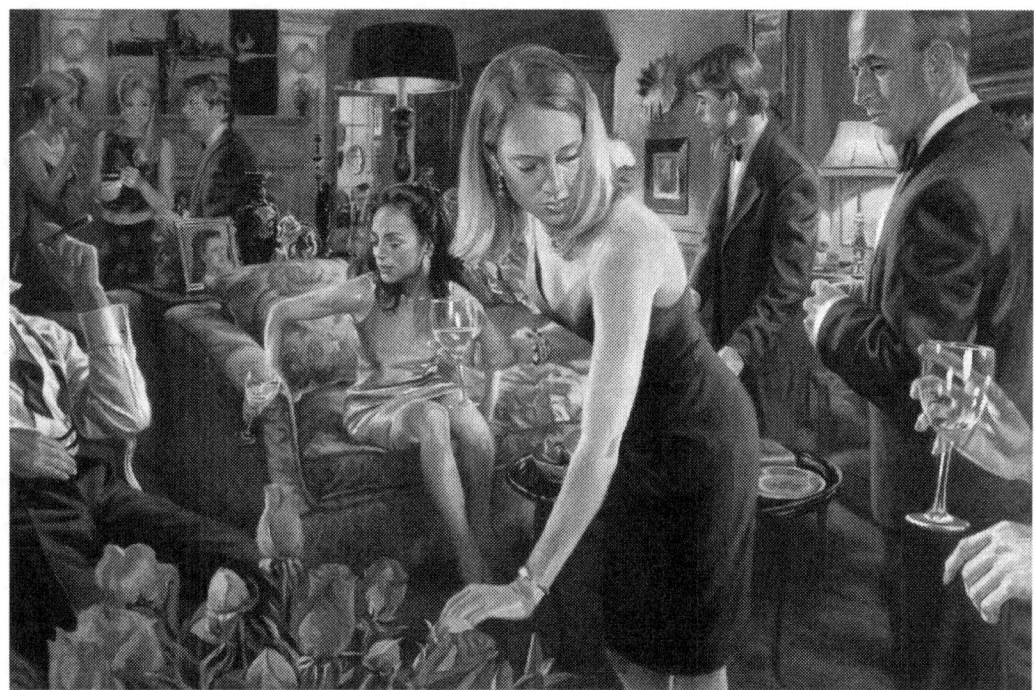

Fig. 27. *Cross Currents* (2000, 57" x 87 ½")

The people depicted in Rodgers' paintings are all lost angels. Compare the grand masters and their angels and prophets and saints. By comparison, Rodgers' angels are lost and looking for something and not likely to find it. It is a recipe for a religion waiting to sweep them up. Enlightenment, fulfillment—it eludes them even as a fantasy. According to Rodgers' conception of things, even people of great power, simultaneously villified or deified by different segments of the population, are essentially innocent because even they can't fully know what's going on. *Cross Currents* comments on religion's packaging of spirituality in the relentlessly material world. Note the painting (the image of the cross) in the left rear. The cross represents many crossed currents of sublimated desire and belief systems gone awry. "If Christ can't do it, no one can," Rodgers says impishly, as if to deflect the seriousness of his examination of culture, religion, and society. As with belief in the church, these figures are all caught up in the web of a belief in their own arbitrarily chosen system. The suggestion is that all of this nicey-nice, decorous costuming, well-put-togetherness is done to suppress natural inclinations as well as to enhance them, to encourage them to be civilized, constrained, well-behaved with each other, and yet this front woman's gentle décolletage was intended to impress the man behind her in his modern suit of armor. So each is in the armor of their part, armor that is meant to both constrain and titillate.

As in later Rodgers' works, the empty glass on the right serves to magnify and distort. It is both lovely, civilized order and sophisticated disorder. The constraint of the entire circus of belief and custom is emphasized by this very domestic setting, complete with paintings, lamps, and photographs. It is all very homey, except that they are putting on their best show of artillery. Pomp and circumstance. As we can see in the upper left, Tapies' symbol of their faith in the system is in flames. Desire is an intersection, a crucifixion, a crux. We are all sentenced to both suffering and vitality in the absolute and most important moment, the present circumstance, which is never what we intend to make of it, no matter how carefully we plan and how well we behave. Desire as a force or idea cannot be proven, and perhaps doesn't actually exist. Maybe, in fact, it is the guise we mask simple human compulsion in. We must do something, so what desires do we desire?

Unsatisfied desire is a tonic, a motivation, a goad. If we can keep it free—independent of mere formality, habit, formula, routine—it can sustain us. Desire is alertness, sensitivity, life. We thrive on the current of desire, on the little vectors being pumped out of us, on the distance and even impossibility of the destination of desire. We are buoyed by little responses, by intermittent reinforcement that sustains our capacity to generate desire. One little vector back at us can keep us going for weeks. Months. Years. And even after there is nothing coming back, we can still live out our desire, but the vectors become feeble, futile, misdirected, and ineffectual. No matter how successful we might have been at one time, eventually we turn our vectors inward, and we feel the sting of their little arrows, reminding us of a lifetime of unfulfilled desire. Because, by definition, desire is that which cannot be fulfilled, and it is that which breeds only itself until it is terminally inbred, weakened, and bled dry of all vitality.

5. Knowing Where We're Going

*"For anyone to claim that they know exactly what they're about
is both a noble notion and a flagrant fiction, and therefore intensely interesting."*
—Terry Rodgers

The idea of knowing where we are going or even where we want to go is a fascinating fantasy, a hopeful fiction, a desperate notion, and, in many cases, a disorienting, preoccupying, possibly destructive distraction from actual life. Rodgers believes this, but he also sees the nobility in it, and his paintings attempt to capture that nobility of personal predicaments as much as the chaos of the counterfeit culture. One of the most profound and most powerful contemporary desires is to have a purpose, to live a meaningful life, and thus to embody "integrity." Yet a coherent, meaningful "direction" ("career" in the sense of a life's trajectory, a calling that sends us in a specific vocational direction) is the vector that so few of us truly embody, enmeshed as we are in hustling and bustling among the dozens of daily vectors associated with going here and there, getting this and that done, and being sure to see all the people we think we are supposed to see while planning the vacations and retirements that are indicated as our birthright and therefore our mandated desire. Even as Americans collectively (and self-congratulatorily) celebrate what is called in group-speak, "our freedoms," an ominous possibility looms in the near future: that a new kind of totalitarianism will emerge, one which constrains us by information, portability, and mobility—one that will weave such an overwhelming and claustrophobic web of choices, options, and opportunities around each of us that we will be paralyzed once and for all.

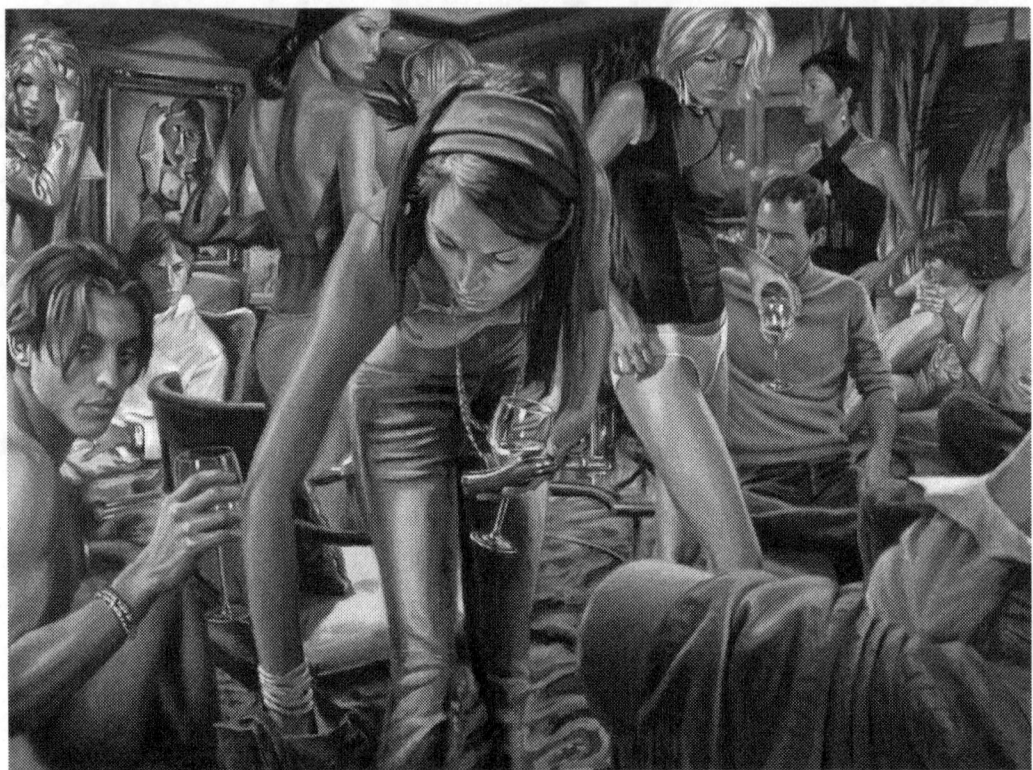

Fig. 28. *The Uncertainty Principle* (2003, 54" x 75")

The Uncertainty Principle highlights the major and minor mysteries of existence and the paradox of choice in a world in which decisiveness is more a studied professional pose than a practical, personal approach to living our lives among numberless, ever-changing variables and conditions. The guy on the left is looking more or less at us, but really past us, as if he smugly sees and knows something we don't. The woman in the center is coming right out at us, leaning into us, in our face, perhaps merely to find her cigarette lighter or her keys. The three women facing generally to our right form a kind of line and create a progressive sensation. The two women in the next plane back are facing the other way, to our left, and are set against the flow suggested by the other three. The two males bracket the central action. All of this flux and all of these contesting vectors stir up a sense of movement and confusion; there is orderly chaos or chaotic order, but we can't tell what the key components of order might be in this world. Desire could well be a motivation common to all of the characters here, but what is the nature of that desire?

Rodgers' work suggests that what we consider to be our own desires are no more nor less than an agenda laid out for us by advertising, promotion, and entertainment media, particularly movies and magazines. Our desires are also increasingly conditioned and limited by the idea of perfectibility. We should look, feel, act, and think in certain prescribed ways, about which we have conflicting ideas because of books, magazines, radio and TV programs, motivational speakers, religious leaders, loved ones, and therapists. For example, in any given day, I could get X, Y, and Z done. I should, in fact. I "want" to—I might say I have a desire to get them done—and yet I don't really want to. By the end of the day, when I have, predictably, not accomplished what I really didn't "want to do," I then consign myself to the category of failure. In fact, I had no idea what I wanted. My desires are vexed, conflicted, and destined to be frustrated. I hide them from myself. Having rejected the myths of religion, and preferred to find our own way, thank you, we have sentenced ourselves to a perpetual walk in the wilderness of confusing temptation. If only there were a single, pure desire to organize my life, I catch myself thinking, I might be more sure of my footing.

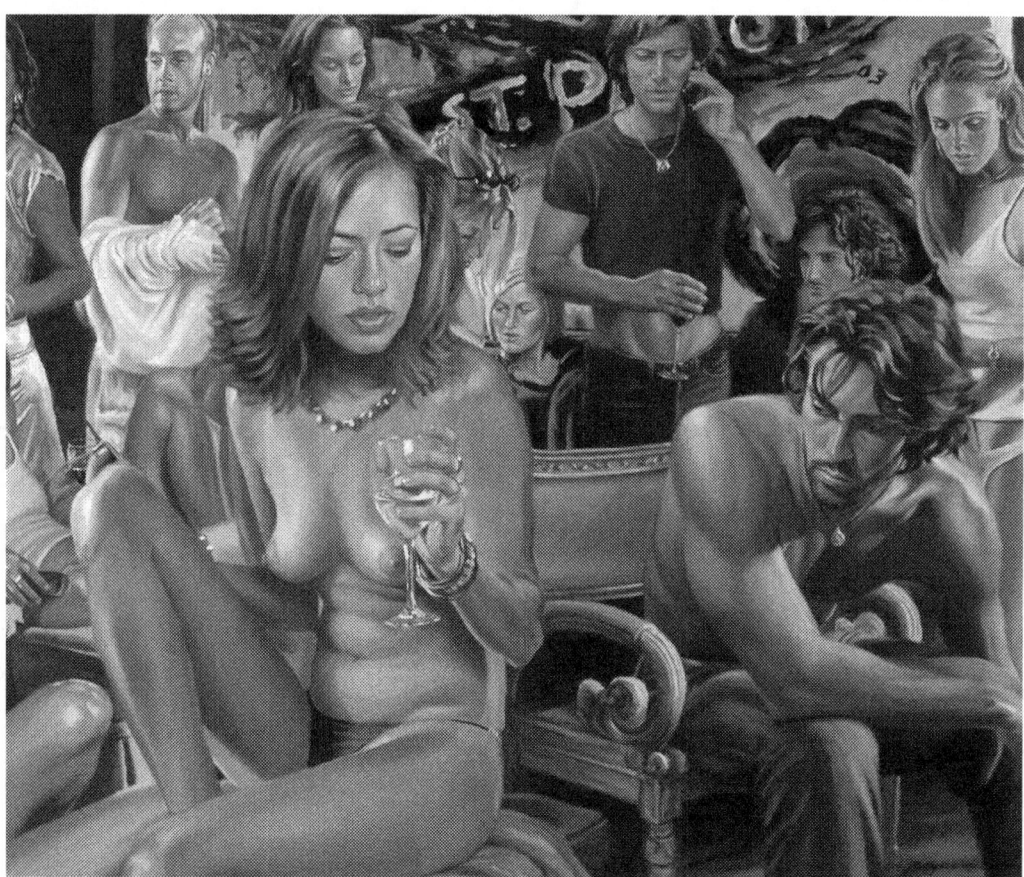

Fig. 29. *Desiderata* (2003, 56" x 67 ½")

Rodgers has addressed the notion of the "desideratum" and its ever-increasing multiples in *Desiderata*. He employs the same Schnabel painting in the background as he did in *American Rhapsody* (an altered *St. Paolo Malfi*), as well as the favorite Rodgerian male model, "Brian," who not only appeared in *American Rhapsody*, but subsequently in *This Is Our Youth* and *Anatomy of Desire* as well as in earlier paintings, such as *Perishable Goods*. Here we see a disordered universe (unlike *Cartesian Coordinates*), something a little like chaos. Characters seem to be groping for a way of being. They are definitely not people with resolved lives. There seems to be confusion on every face, and the male in the center background could be on the line for help. So many phones show up in Rodgers: symbols of disconnection, wishes for connection, and palpable separateness and transience. But maybe the desire "to get away," to escape, is the strongest desire of all—to be anywhere but where we are. "To be here or to be there" has taken over from "to be or not to be." This painting has the feel of a circus, or the sign on the side of a circus wagon, indicating a place to escape from our boring lives, as if there are performers here (the girl on the right, the guy pulling on or off his shirt as if to change costumes between performances). "Nothing is out of place but the people," Rodgers observes.

And the people are dislocated by their haunting suspicion that they could be somewhere even better, doing something even more hip. American advertising is famously the art of manufacturing unsatisfiable desire. This endless artificial desire isn't "primary," in the sense that it isn't a basic human appetite, but it is continuously reinforced by cultural conditioning and carefully linked to the more fundamental human appetites, which can lead to odd but intentional combinations of behaviors, such as excessive exercising instead of eating, or excessive eating instead of working, or excessive Internet surfing instead of anything else. It can end in complete psychic confusion regarding the spatial and temporal dimensions of human experience as well as the physiological and moral. The tension and suspense of possibility and postponement can increase the force of desire. Rodgers educes the sense of time and space in such a way that Marvell comes to mind: "Had we world enough and time...." And sometimes the scenes Rodgers shows us smack of too much world and too much time, not to mention insufficient coyness (except perhaps on the part of the painter himself). In any case, no matter how great the degree of disorientation (or perhaps because of it), we don't want to miss out on any part of the great party that is going on in the culture day and night.

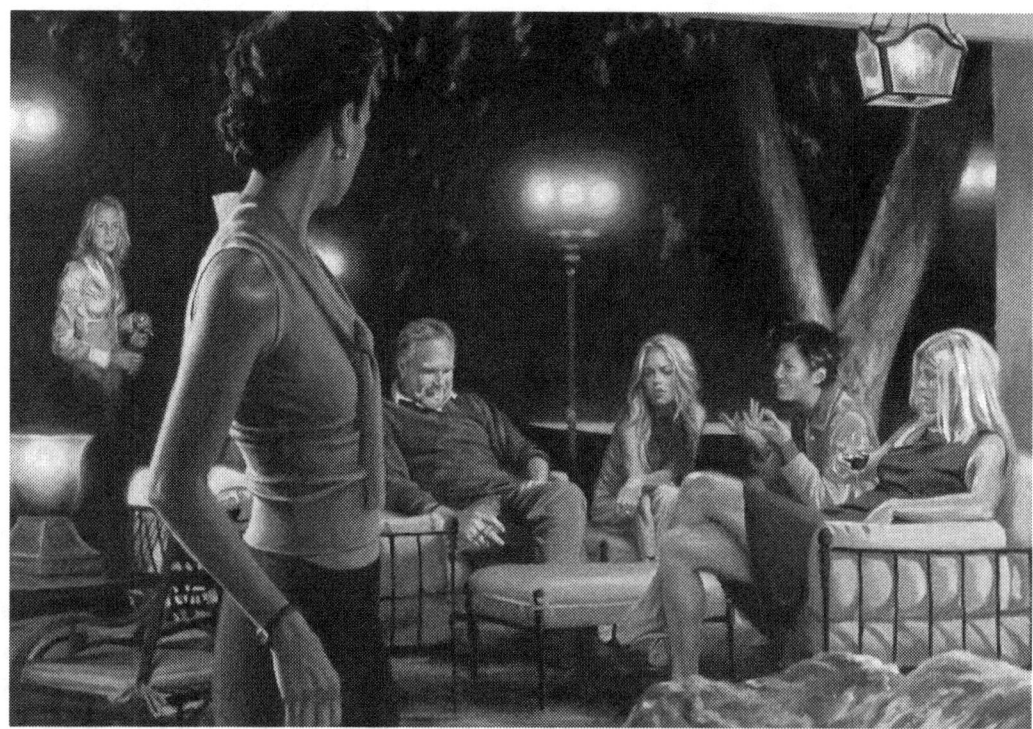

Fig. 30. *Night Vision* (2003, 50" x 74")

In wartime, with new technology, military forces have the capacity to see in the dark, which is something that would come in handy to the Rodgers characters whose lives seem to be lived there. *Night Vision* is an artificial situation, out-of-doors, well after dark, with everything very well-lighted—almost too well-lighted. The vectors of light illuminate them, the satyr and his nymphs, this most happy-seeming harem, in this apparently natural, relaxed, comfortable setting, but how do we make sense of the one guy with the five women his age or younger? There is so much light shed on so much darkness, and yet so little enlightenment. They seem to be passing the time; that's all we can say. The figure in the foreground, whose face we cannot see (and whose mind we cannot read) serves as our escort into a situation where another standing figure looking toward her suggests that there might be something else going on that the seated figures, all happy and relaxed, aren't aware of. The seated woman on the right is so tall that her legs stretch out into the constellation of characters in a way that unsettles the composition. The suggestion of the title points us toward things that cannot be seen with the unaided eye, potentially dangerous things. But we don't have the means at our disposal to see what might be there.

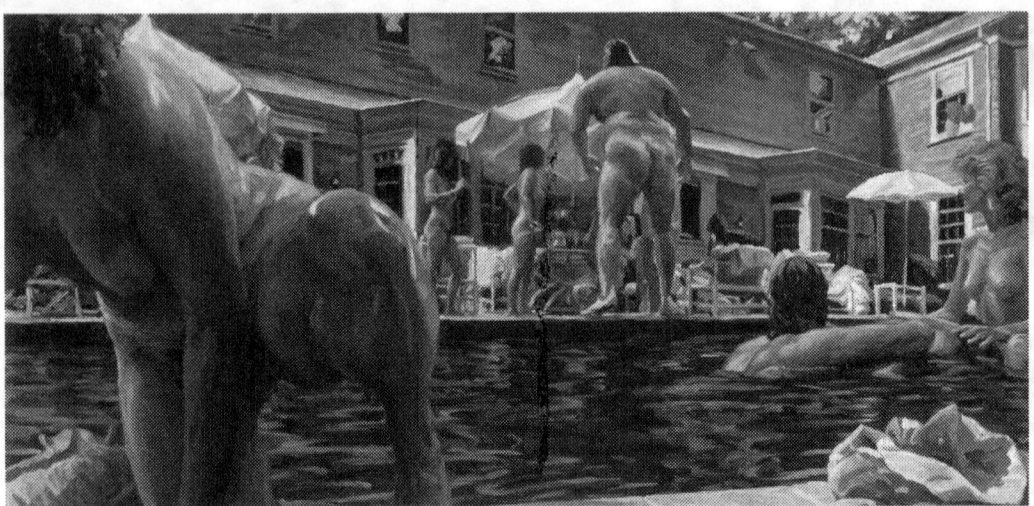

Fig. 31. *Dana's Pool* (1991, 60" x 128")

Similarly, our vision is obstructed in *Dana's Pool,* a scene of great but inexact poolside spectacle, in which, if we allow our eye to take us wherever it goes, enjoying the humor of the exposed and exaggerated human forms, we are slow to realize that something is really not right. And, even by Rodgers' standards, the canvas is enormous, over ten feet across. Much of this picture directs us to an incident beneath the center umbrella, an unknown incident that is entirely unidentifiable, but so many of the participants are focused on it. Whatever is happening is obscured by the naked backside of a man. The thrust of the picture's organization takes us almost into the house because of the lines at the far back right, but the figure that grabs the viewer's attention is the huge naked one climbing out of the pool in the front left because she's so completely in our face, so that we're torn back and forth between the sexuality (the voyeuristic prurience) and some other concern, which is presumably serious. This is a disturbing scene; something has happened in the background. The foreground is entirely visceral, so that there is a dynamic, even dominant push-pull. Though Rodgers rejects any interest in or influence by Pearlstein—"Poussin, more likely, or even Degas!" Rodgers laughs—he could be seen to be playing with Pearlstein's conceptions of the human form, adding muscle and tissue for an effect that is at the same time exposed and unusually strong. There is a monumental quality, like some of Picasso's early figures, but not as airy and light as Picasso's; these people seem heavily-burdened by their very persons, and the entire scene is bathed in a murkiness that is simultaneously atmospheric, moral, and spiritual, with dark muddy colors everywhere, and not a single bright, clear, primary color in evidence. The murkiness enhances the mystery of the scene, and, from the viewer's point of view, intellectually, it accents a typical Rodgerian interrogation: What am I looking at, what is going on, what am I looking for, where is all of this headed, and to what extent am I seeing only what I want to see? And is my life like this, characterized by incident that I don't recognize or can't interpret? Something has gone wrong, is all that we know, most of the time.

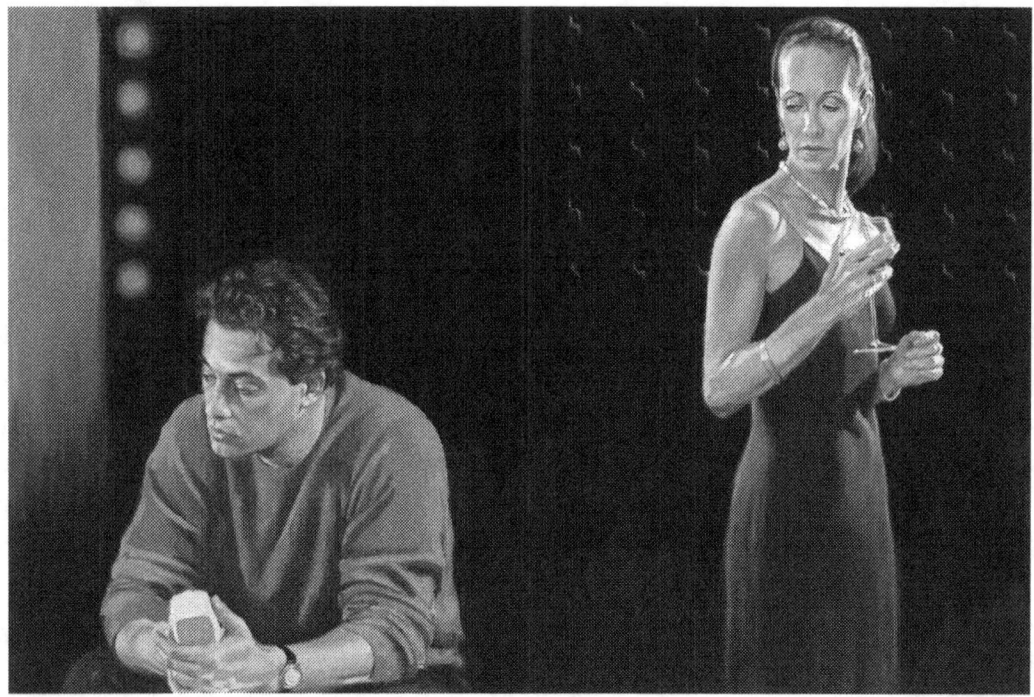

Fig. 32. *Damaged Kingdom* (2002, 48" x 74")

Damaged Kingdom suggests that once upon a time someone had something that was splendid, but now it is flawed—chillingly flawed. This is a shockingly spare and severe Rodgers painting, and one of his few duos. It is immediately apparent that this is a stylized version of the struggle to communicate in the contemporary world. There is a contrast between the very real rendition of the couple's physicality and their mental state as they interact (however coldly) in this futuristic space that is almost graphic, approximating pure symbol, but could be a room with green lights that are blurred from a distance, in the way that so many contemporary buildings have illumination or architecture that has a certain grid-like regularity involving tiles and lights.

Rodgers extrapolates that tendency to the Nth degree. The result is a high-tech, sterile space. There is a decided contrast between real human experience and the constructed world and all of its inhuman elements. One wonders where they thought they were headed when they arrived here. The standing woman has a drink, while the seated, depressed-looking male wears a watch and holds an apparently recently-used telephone: one more aspect of the digital, non-human world as well as a futile medium of communication. There is a huge chasm between the rarefied world of global communication and the story of what goes on between the two of them. Clearly, the phone is no help when it comes to communicating with her. There is an entire set of narrative possibilities for what is going on between them, and her expression and posture denote suspicion and coldness, possibly presaging her imminent departure. The useless phone may represent a whole range of compulsions and addictions that undermine our relationships and threaten our mental health, even while promising us happiness. The man is clinging to the telephone, having committed himself to a world in which the communications from afar are privileged over those more proximate. In this "damaged kingdom," intimacy is now easier by voice contact than by body contact.

Part of what Rodgers concerns himself with and thereby presents to the viewer is what the novelist David Foster Wallace, that expert on addiction, explains: "…it is often more fun to want something than to have it." Wallace adds that others can see more about us than we can see about ourselves and implies that we are all addicts of one sort or another, further noting that addicts' relationships are "provisional." With people, we have trouble; with objects, we're fine. We're all consumption addicts now. The nineteenth century was characterized by the disease known as "consumption" that was about breathing; our twenty-first century malady is about being. We can relate better to salespeople than we do to our loved ones. Freedom and democracy turn out to be more about material acquisition than about human expression and relation.

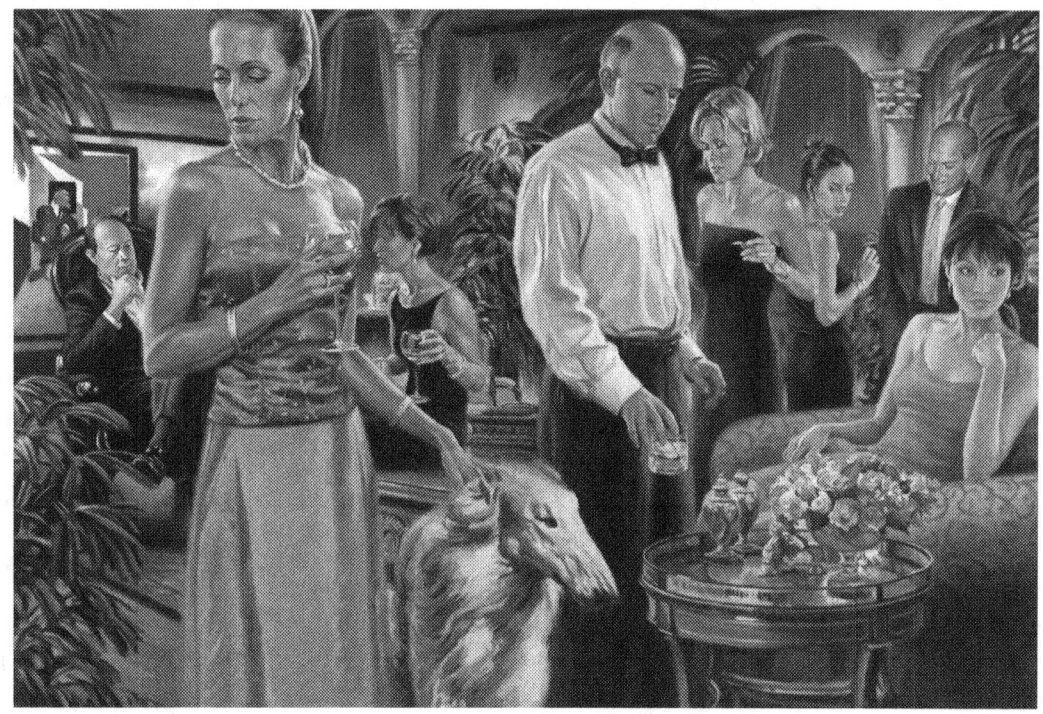

Fig. 33. *The Grammar of Democracy* (2002, 52" x 78")

The Grammar of Democracy presents us with two high-end status symbols: another Francis Bacon painting (Rodgers uses one in *The Dialogues* as well) and fashion designer Oscar de la Renta, in person. Like Paris Hilton, de la Renta is a symbol of something much more than he is a merely present person, but the title suggests that this painting reveals something about the rules of that great American political and market economy under the practically mythological notion of "democracy." It's a careful crowd here, as Americans increasingly discover themselves to be, apparently feeling ill-at-ease in general, and perhaps inadequate to their surroundings and their exalted company. The woman in the red bustier looks extremely ill-at-ease, perhaps relying on the dog to keep her balance, and this is a realization of an awkward interior moment for more than one person. Although it's an awfully elegant setting—and we can't know if it's public or private—the implication of the Bacon painting suggests it's a private domain. In the midst of this very fancy private party, the two principal figures seem to radiate consternation. Her attention is so clearly away; his could be with hers, but hers couldn't be with him. The blonde is in her own world, completely oblivious to what's around her. The redhead and man on the left are in a conversation, as is de la Renta. Two couples are involved in doing something, and other people are trapped inside their own heads. The presence of the dog suggests the odd contrast between another form of life and the human social system. And immediately after you think of the dog as a different form of life, you see that it is a highly-cultivated, highly-bred acquisition for some human. Certain kinds of dogs and cats represent achievement. Just another branded experience. This dog is not generic or natural at all—a very specialized breed, it costs a lot, like a Prada purse or a de la Renta suit. One acquires the dog in conjunction with one's other carefully calibrated purchases. And the animal is an integral part of the constrained, packaged, manipulated natural world, not only owned and well-trained, but with genetics managed, like the plants and like the people—they're all reined in, or, if they hold the reins, like Oscar, they are reining themselves in. The plants are also precisely-fitted accouterments, luxuriantly spreading their fronds as if to naturalize this extraordinarily artificial environment, this extravagantly-designed space appropriate to the upper echelon of human experience, with its antique (or imitation antique) tea table, and the kind of painting that mirrors the finely-tuned angst in this space of sharp angles and phony columns. The whole physical confection functions as a kind of lens through which to misread the world, or to see the world in tinted glasses, at the very least, discoloring and prejudicing everything in a certain way, so as not to inconveniently discomfort anyone.

And what if we were to recognize ourselves just a little bit in such a scene? That's the possibility the viewer risks in most of these paintings. This one is a kind of question, "a conundrum," as Rodgers likes to put it, that foregrounds the upscale human dilemma: Why are we here, and how are we to behave, given that we have nothing to go on but these highly-generalized myths that are primarily helpful in their suggestion of specific purchases? (I know what to acquire; I just don't know exactly why.) In fact, Rodgers' people avoid more than they seek, as if what they sought has brought them to a place where they are in danger, either physical danger or, more commonly, emotional or spiritual danger. The desire to be safe, sure, on solid ground comes to the fore. Many seem caught in a half-realized web of self-consciousness, fixed and doomed, waiting, "held as if on pause," as Lilly Wei puts it (*Terry Rodgers,* Fay Gold Gallery, 2002). Perhaps the next purchase will solve the dilemma.

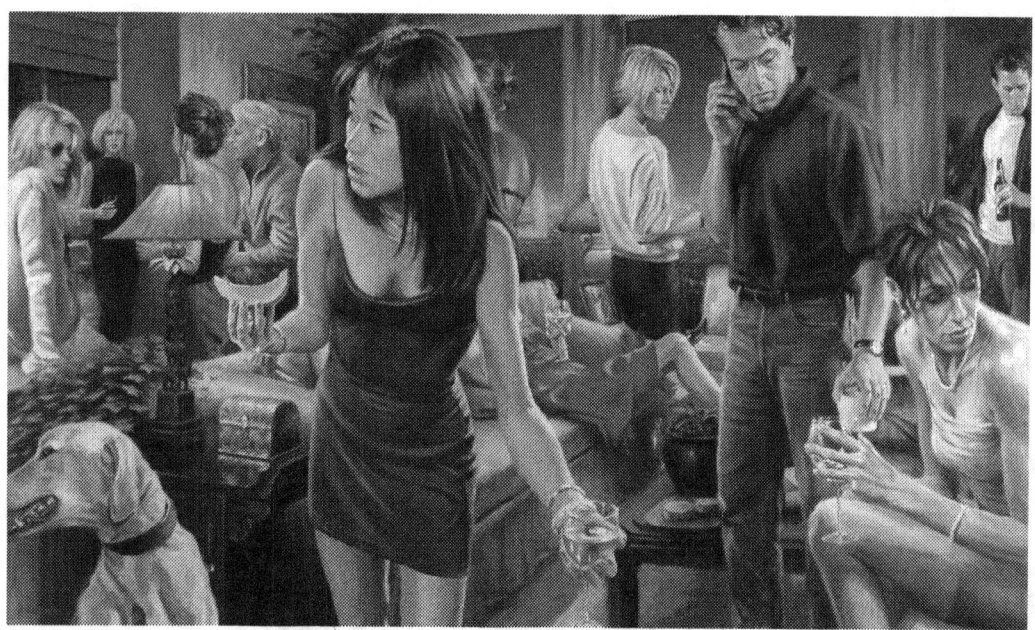

Fig. 34. *Buying Time* (2001, 48" x 83")

Buying Time includes a central character frozen in the midst of plenty, trapped with no next move in mind. When in doubt, buy something, anything. In our culture, Rodgers observes, it's always time to buy. Much care has been taken in the acquisition of the house, the clothing, and even the dog. The grouping in the left rear seems to be in some kind of comparatively comfortable engagement, but the rest of the people are looking awkwardly in different directions. The woman in the center reaches for her wine even as she holds a piece of melon. Her predicament represents the fact of our having too much stuff. There is an underlying awkwardness and discomfort in a cultural situation where we have at our disposal too much of a good thing: too much opportunity, too many possessions, and much more than enough "plenty." The male figure with the phone is escaping to some other mental place or space, either through making or receiving a call, or simply by checking his messages, replaying old messages, or even absolutely faking some marginal engagement in order not to have to be involved with anyone actually present. The woman in red on the couch seems to be alone, and her isolation and alienation is emphasized by the fact that her head is obscured from view; only her body is present. Everyone is trying to get by, buying time until they can find something actual, safe, substantial, or—impossible to imagine—meaningful. Meaningful action, thought, or companionship seems unlikely, except possibly in the left rear portion of the painting, where the more removed figures prevent us from ascertaining just how engaged the participants are (though certainly they are more engaged than the closer ones). This looks like the kind of party where everyone has come to sell but might content themselves to be sold. If we are buying or selling, we are more easily able to slip into a purposeful mode, perhaps even a pleasurable mode. But anything outside of the commercial mode, anything purely personal, is a vexed subject. The woman has no one to sell to or buy from at the moment. She is awkwardly situated on her own, waiting to find the opportunity to "hook up" in some kind of way, to make the party work for her. She's managed to occupy her hands but not her mind. This painting juxtaposes the pure and simple desire of the dog with the wariness of the woman who looks in the same direction, but what she sees is no clear path to anything, just a blur of possible avenues to an uncertain future, which might be even more awkward than this present moment.

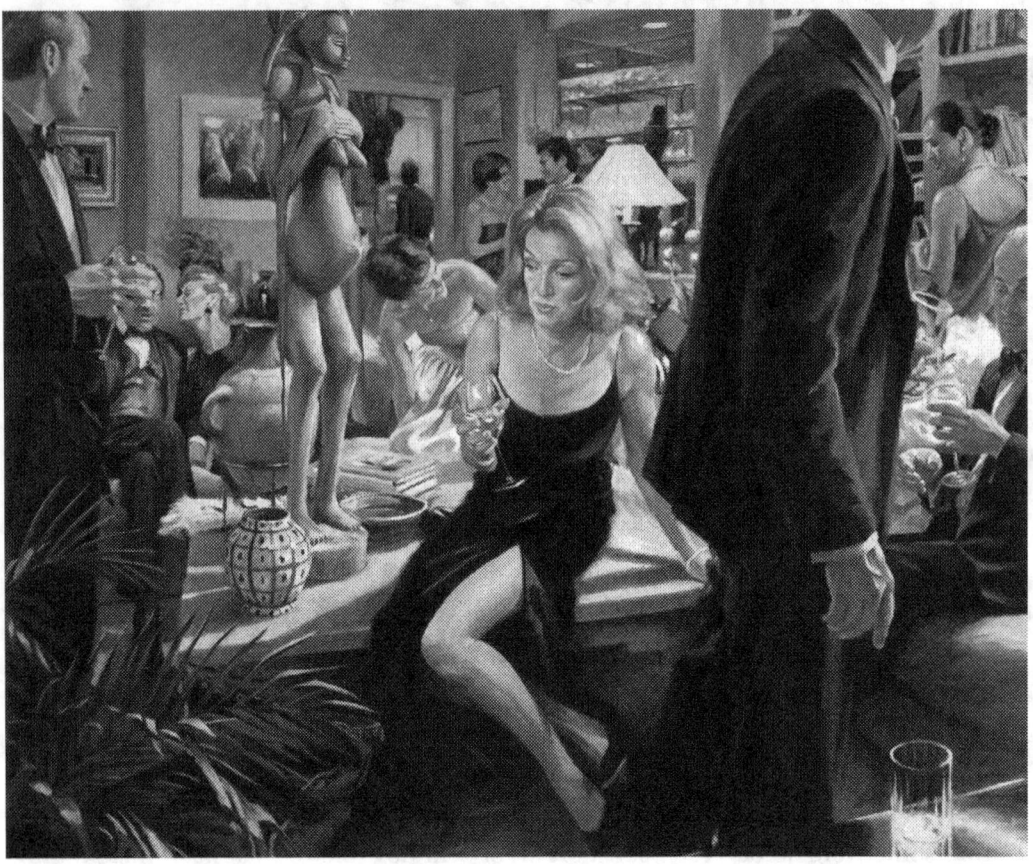

Fig. 35. *The Exchange* (1997, 60" x 75")

The Exchange scrutinizes another such character, a female figure who seems to have lost everything just in the moment of the picture. An exchange is an intersection: vectors crossing, vectors crossed, forces at cross purposes, influencing one another, perhaps unequally. There are personal and cultural intersections and exchanges in this painting. Like a stock exchange, values are fluctuating, deals are made, and the chaos of the forces is packaged in some kind of civilized, highly-commercialized system that masks the primal emotions and motives: greed, desperation, brutality, and every opportunistic instinct known to man(un)kind. The apparent African fertility image dominates this painting. The wooden sculpture stands on a coffee table and constitutes the middle ground, around which the social activity swirls. In the lower left, an expansive houseplant suggests a jungle in which rich and mysterious alien life forms might be hiding. There are various women who echo the wooden figure, but in contemporary, formal, Western party garments. The sublimated suburban civilization runs up against the ostensibly natural contrasting figure, which is itself an abstraction and idealization of female nature, a fictive embodiment of imagination and superstition.

There is an obvious contrast with the blonde in the black dress, partially displaying her body and clearly unhappy with the result of this highly cultured and comparatively advanced moment in human history. She could be disappointed, drunk, or even shattered in some life-changing way. It is as if the African sculpture observes and accepts or even invites the emotional nakedness and the calamity of human progress. This painting hints more at some superstitious ritual involving Armani suits, designer dresses, and complicated but very trivially-based emotions. The fecundity of the traditional values from some distant (and perhaps lost) society contrasts with the sterility of the scientifically-advanced society. The dark male figure could have caused that look on the woman's face. He's like a passing cloud, like the one she's dealing with (not necessarily the cause or occasion). Or perhaps it's the certain knowledge, the fatal knowledge, that her own days of fecundity are finished, and that what remains for her is a status of continually diminishing proportions.

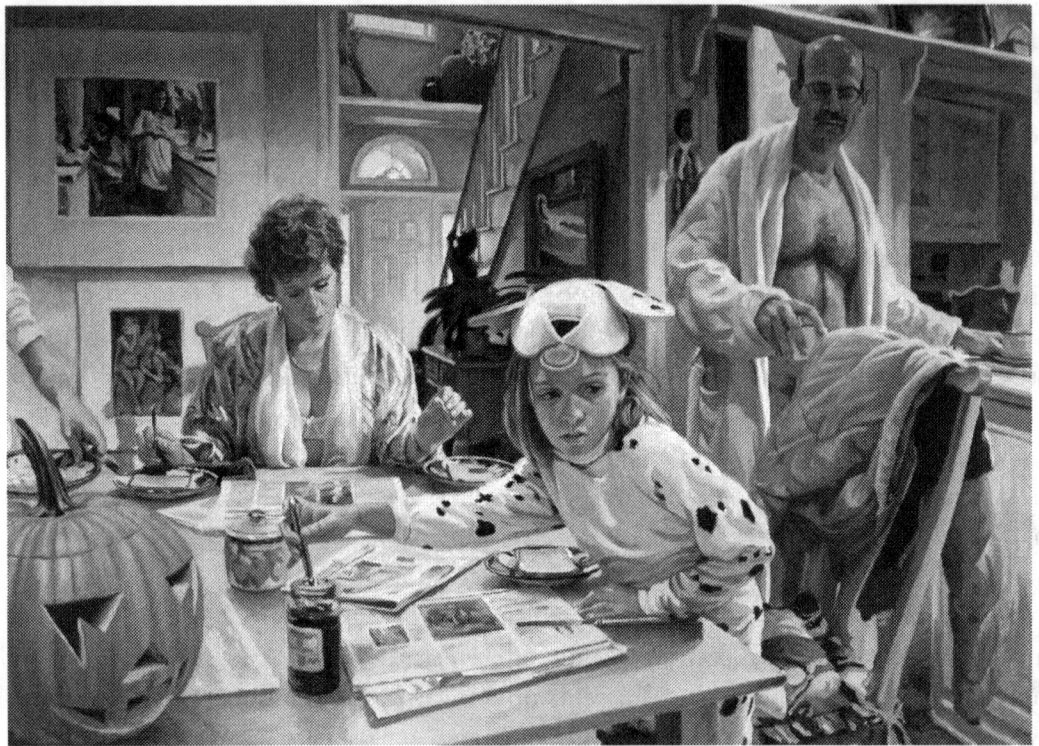

Fig. 36. *Halloween Breakfast* (1997, 54" x 77")

Halloween Breakfast may be Rodgers' most direct examination of the American dream as it has materialized and stagnated in white, suburban culture. Everything is both right and wrong in this scene. Leisure and abundance are represented in a hundred ways, but so is the sinister extrapolation of plenty, the corruption of too-much-ness, and the vestigal hegemony of a patriarchy characterized by brutal opportunistic habit. Halloween, one of the perennially favorite American holidays among children and adolescents, is also the celebration of ghoulishness, terror, and death.

Richard Vine, the managing editor and writer for *Art in America*, has written that this painting "exudes latent sexuality where we both expect and disapprove of it most: in the family. In an upper middle-class kitchen, a middle-aged couple in bathrobes read the newspaper and take their morning coffee—she with her ample breasts partially showing, he with his robe hanging open and his genitalia nonchalantly exposed, though a chair back just hides them from our view. Their young daughter, wearing a Dalmatian costume (a pop-culture sign for threatened innocence), reaches across the table (to dip a knife in a jar of red jam!) with a backward turn of the head that suggests an "unmasked" mistrust of the father behind her. A sexual dynamic animates the space itself, as it simultaneously zooms back and thrusts forward in the middle of picture plane, carrying our attention, willy-nilly, up the stairs toward the unseen bedrooms above. What strange disguises and disrobings, what childish games, we wonder, haunt this morning repast?"

In the Rodgers oeuvre, this painting owes most to genre painting or narrative, and yet we feel uncomfortable asking where this is going. The little girl is dipping into something dangerous. The cute Dalmatian is at the mercy of forces she will perhaps never understand, no matter how much analysis she subsequently endures. It is the sad, archetypical American family with symbolic threats looming everywhere, including the jack o' lantern. Compartmentalization is a tactic that people employ to avoid the real issues. The room itself is all compartmentalized. There is a doorway from the kitchen into next room, another doorway to the outdoors, a staircase leading up to some other realm (probably even more dangerous), a cabinet to the right, the obligatory American kitchen island, more cabinets to the right of the standing man, and a door probably to the basement downstairs, another unknown, dark, and troubling realm. There are two photographs, images of children, and some sort of painting over the little girl that includes someone who is nude. There are compartments of paintings, compartments of their heads where their thoughts arise and are kept, and numerous other separate spaces that suggest secrets and forgotten knowledge. Then there is the little table with drawers between little girl and woman, boxes and spaces and holding patterns—everything is in a holding pattern—and thank goodness it is because it looks like it could all go wrong at any minute if anything were turned loose. It's a real scene of naturalism: coat over chair, papers strewn on table, partly empty jelly jar, slightly open robes. There is the somber effect of the shadows and the eyes with all of these divided-up images suggesting an infinitude of threats, fears, and suppression/repression/near depression, and then of course the ridiculous permanently-smiling pumpkin, the false face on it all—an evil, sadistic suggestion of some demon that shadows this household and others just like it.

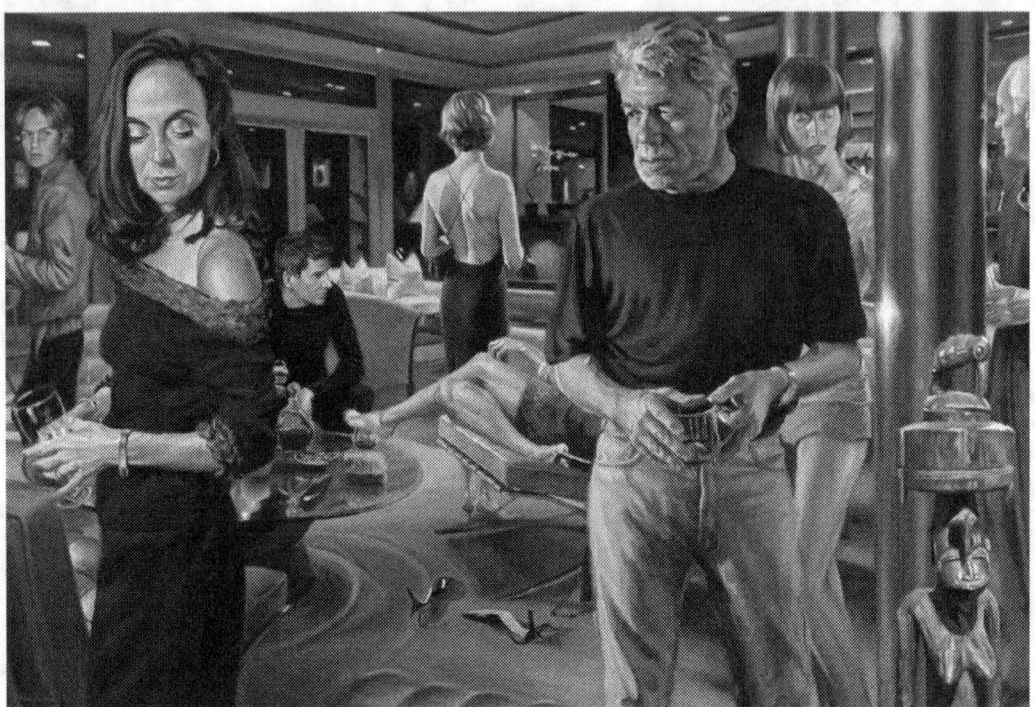

Fig. 37. *The Declension of Time* (2001, 48" x 73")

Unlike many artists, Rodgers is not the typical bourgeoisophobe, to use a term that Flaubert applied to himself. "Those days are gone," he says, "or they should be." He believes that the idea of the pure artist, completely alienated from the bourgeoisie is yet another construct, and a self-serving one at that, as far as contemporary artists are concerned. Rodgers also sees high culture and popular culture as indistinguishable now. "All of those wishful distinctions are passé," he says. All culture is suspect, susceptible to corruption, and obviously decaying before our eyes when we see it in a Rodgers painting, such as the *The Declension of Time*. The title is reminiscent of T.S. Eliot's line in *Four Quartets*: Time past and time future. In the severe and modern high-rise loft with glinting metallic poles, as some of the characters begin to show their age, we end up watching a dance that seems like some sort of ritualized sexuality. Everybody looks their version of the best they can, calling up some aspect of their physical attractiveness: tigers on the prowl in a very stylish contemporary cage. There is play between the conventions of allure but also this indication of lofts or apartments ad infinitum, suggested by the windows against the dark, and the suggestion of both primitive sexuality and primitive interpretations, styles of adornment, or superstition, worlds with alien cultures going infinitely in two directions. Nothing is resolved, but the certainty of the styles remains the same, the convictions about the styles, and the commitment to them. As Rodgers puts it, "Too often, it's stronger than any religious faith." Perhaps this observation might also explain how funadamentalist and extremist religious faiths, predicated on resistance to a global, transcultural tendency, overcompensate with such force that they wind up resorting to apocalyptic stratagems.

Notwithstanding his willingness to include himself among the ever-villified bourgeoisie—"Isn't everyone acting bourgeois nowadays?"—Rodgers himself is an unreconstructed bohemian who wears jewelry and is quite adept at sewing together a split seam in his wife's skirt at breakfast. And he is quick to call attention to what he considers "the surprisingly deep-seated conservatism of this supposedly advanced culture." Rodgers sees in the queasy, uneasy responses to his paintings by gallery-goers a clear indication that "people still think nudity is somehow a moral issue." As an aficionado of the beaches at St. Tropez, of which he has made extensive photographic and sketch records, not to mention more than a dozen brilliant paintings, Rodgers revels in nudity and deeply enjoys the various tones of human skin and the endless shapes of human bodies, even in the most unlikely combinations.

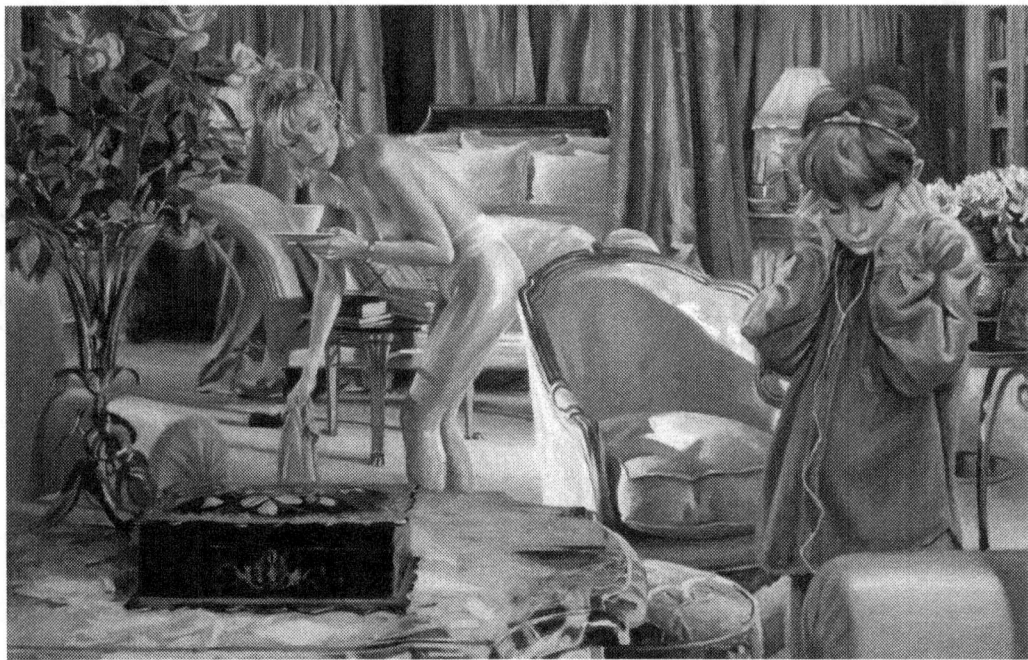

Fig. 38. *Hear No Evil* (1999, 48" x 78")

One such jolting juxtaposition occurs in *Hear No Evil*. There is a woman, half-clothed, and a child with headphones. The palette is the same screechingly decorative one Rodgers used in *Boyz II Men* and *And Then There Were None*, and it is applied to similarly troubling subject matter. The lavender spot among the gold, the slightest hint of rose in the couch directly behind her, and the curtains, air and the marble slab table in the foreground are rich with gilded colors. The blue is not very strong—it has a muddy quality. The purple she's picking up sings out. A lot of things point to her. This is vectoral delight, pointing in narrative and thematic directions that speak to social and cultural dead ends, if not absolute doom. The child could be a boy or a girl, but it seems less important than in some Rodgers works. More than most of the other paintings, though the figures are obviously central, they show up as almost incidental in the fullness and lushness of the picture. This is one of the most spatially complex paintings: the chair between the two of them has more going on in it than in many paintings (curve, puff of pillow, wood, light that goes across, the shadow encased inside, slight variable reflections in satiny brocade surface, clear rendition of chair but complex in terms of its constituents). The entire picture is a continuation of that kind of complexity, including the floor with its dark parts, light parts, shadow parts, and the marble chest top's hodgepodge of colored marble bits. Then there are the leaves, the curtain in the background that breaks up into a four-poster style bed. Within this incredibly opulent reflective surface, this rich, lush, endless, borderless kind of environment, we see these two figures in their uncertain relationship, suggesting both sexuality and innocence. We assume it's a mother and child, with the child completely self-absorbed. We don't know what is going on at that moment, although her posture suggests that she could be calling to a child who does not hear. But something is going on; the insistent opulence, the lushness, makes it more than nothing. There's something going on by the very implication of the sensuality of the space and the overblown nature of the indulgent materiality that almost guarantees a lack of self-awareness because the strain of operating in that hyper-constructed environment precludes natural or genuine feeling and behavior. And in this case a viewer can't possibly dodge the question asked by this painting, even though we may be less inclined to see ourselves enacting such a scene. Voyeurism and class distinctions aside, we are faced with the inevitable cultural and social questions that boil down to, "Where are we going?"

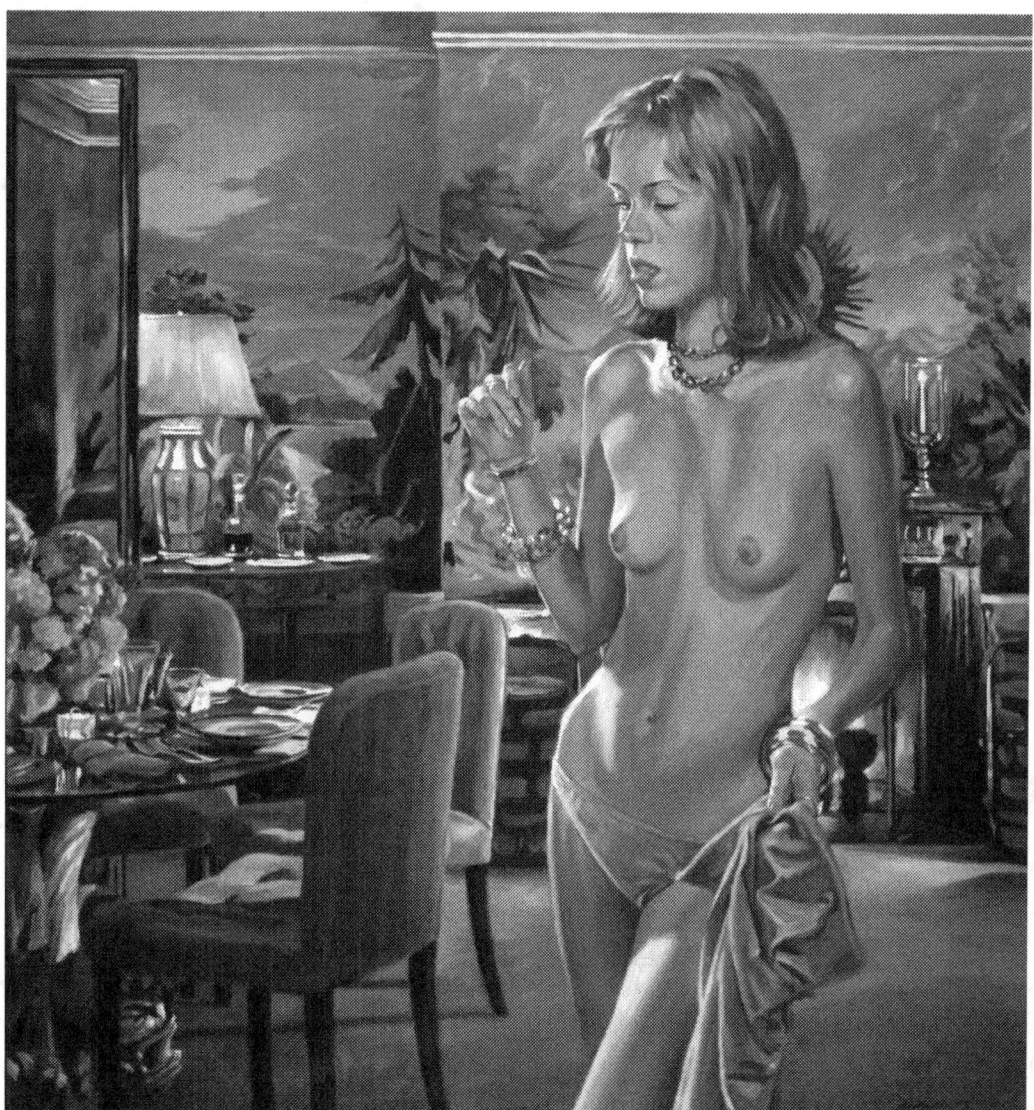

Fig. 39. *The Labyrinth* (2003, 60" x 58")

Even after seeing dozens of Rodgers' works as powerfully disturbing as *Hear No Evil*, and experiencing the discontinuities and puzzlements they generate, to come upon *The Labyrinth* hanging in the artist's home in Columbus, Ohio is to experience a radical dislocation in time and space. Although Rodgers lives in a large home jam-packed with art objects of all shapes, sizes, and media, this painting draws attention to itself and obliterates its surroundings. Unlike any of the photographic images of the painting (in a brochure and on the website), the canvas itself is so rich and dense and darkly vivid as to pull the viewer into another world in which the woman's body blends completely with her surroundings. All of the tones match and merge; all of the textures weave themselves into what feels like a tapestry that communicates depth, history, and high culture, even as it calls into question those very constructs.

This remarkable painting is unusual in the Rodgers oeuvre both because of its single-figure subject and its comparative verticality. In many ways it is a perfect painting, not the least because it seems to collapse the entire known and made world into a very narrow frame. The design of the painting is diabolically clever, and the execution is brilliant. On top of all that, and despite the seeming flatness of the composition, this is one of the paintings in which Rodgers began to apply the depth and dimensionality of his beach pictures to interior scenes, even without the multiple figures that can enhance the appearance of receding distance and various planes of space. Rodgers characterizes this simultaneous flatness and depth as a "double trompe l'oeil," in which the counterfeit dimensionality of the mural on the walls in the background echoes the trickery of three-dimensionality offered to us in the figure and the foreground space.

The young woman's face speaks of formality and even stodginess, echoing her environment, and her body speaks of something else—being free, "tribal" even. There is so much going on, at the simplest level, and at levels too complicated to notice when first viewing the painting. There is a triple contrast between her flesh-and-blood presence, the elaborately-designed room, and the completely fictitious landscape represented on the wall. There is a painted three-dimensional person and a pointedly painted surface, an esthetic joke, and the mural wall has its own three-dimensionality, its own laboratory of pictorial devices. The wall mural landscape deals with monumental spaces and some historic-romantic metaphor, in contrast with the very immediate tactile presence of a person for whom that entire experience may be irrelevant and foreign.

This place may be her mother's or father's or grandparents'—it was definitely put together by someone of an earlier generation's sensibility. She represents the coming into one's own of somebody from a different mindset, and this picture makes it very evident that she's coming into her own completely surrounded by if not repressed by that older generation and conception. This picture depicts her in such a way that we cannot tell the degree to which she wants to overthrow it or resist it, but the way the picture looks it seems that it's a moment when she's conscious of the choice. Her nakedness could be perfectly natural (getting dressed to go out with her parents), or it could be contrary to anything they would allow if they knew. The suggestion is going both ways because we can't tell. The nature of the tentative gesture that she's caught within suggests all of this. There is an ironic, almost comic element in this dramatic skyscape, in this very homey fire burning in the fireplace, and in this very social dining table set for company. What we see is an almost cartoon-like water-monster fish-creature whose tail is holding up the table, monstrous fish face with teeth bared like a demon, which is clearly within that world and within her mind.

Ultimately, the trick of this painting is the way that it blends desirable qualities of cultures past and present, and insinuates the ideal of youthful, slender female perfection into the mix. All women are measured by a few types of female body, and all of those few types are young, svelte, and flawless. We are trapped in a labyrinth from which there is no apparent escape. We can no longer get out, and we must despair of being rescued. We have condemned ourselves to an endlessly brutal classification of people according to arbitrary—and impossible—standards of appearance. The elderly Yeats comes to mind, in all of the poignancy of his confessional lechery. Although "a feeling of wisdom and pure contemplation" was what the poet "always desired," in "The Tower" he spoke of being "lured" into "the labyrinth of another's being"—a being like that of the young woman captured here.

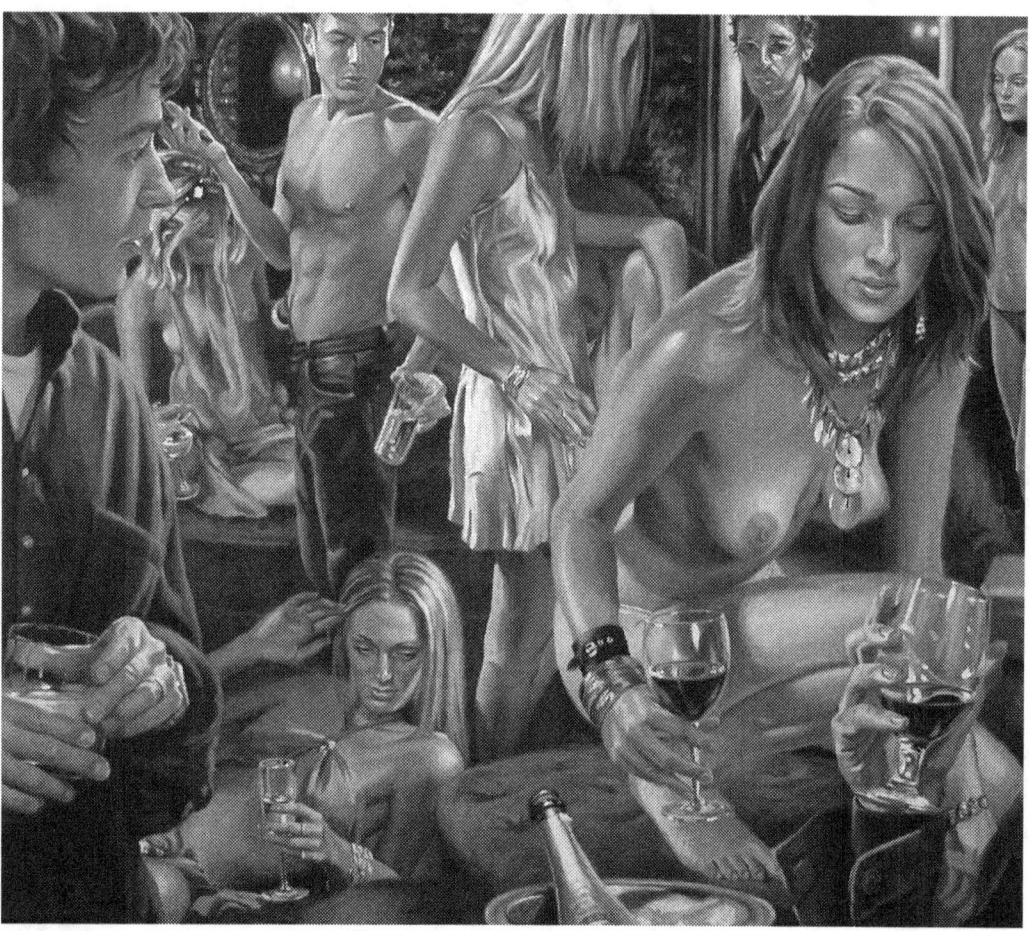

Fig. 40. *En Passant* (2003, 57" x 66")

It is fascinating to compare a dense Rodgers painting like *En Passant* with *The Labyrinth*. From the delicate gesture and slightly anxious serenity of *The Labyrinth*, one moves to *En Passant*, and it feels like being tossed from a quiet pond to Grand Central Station at rush hour. The intense activity is in a plush environment like a car on The Orient Express. People are engaged, but something about the sum total of everything is that it's more than congested—it's intense. Everything is in flux, including even the people in seeming repose. Note the interaction between the mental-facial awarenesses and the movement of the painting: of mind and matter. The depths and dimensions are compressed. One's eye can travel so many steps back into the picture. The eye can move and move and move. Like so many of Rodgers' recent works, this a vectoral paradise. What our eyes and our brains desire is to have this opportunity. Girls are introspective, and guys are just spectators. One looks like a predator. We see women's stereotypical, perhaps genetic interiority. But the guy on the left is caught in a very delicate moment of uncertainty. He is really what the picture is about: regardless of the seeming exterior nature of these people, what actually goes on might be more like this guy, something tentative even in the predator. He's not acting with force, certainty, or clarity. He is merely noticing and not acting, in the middle of judging and responding to his own judgment, thinking, "What could she think of me?" He is an innocent, with his constrained, careful hands mirroring his face, caught in the moment of complete physical *in*activity and mental activity, assessing something, literally trying to get a grip. We can more easily identify with him, and look at the scene through his thoughts. The front right girl's nakedness purports to be revelatory, as if it gets beneath the surface, but in fact she seems less than penetrable. Not accessible, not revealed. Her body is not a whole lot different from clothing; her body is her clothing. Whereas the guy seems accessible, revealed. The least dressed person, paradoxically, is not revealed, and the most dressed person is vulnerable, exposed, and available to interpretation. She is a natural creature; he is a product of civilization. She seems gently protected, and he does not.

The term *en passant* not only connotes the literal translation of "in passing" (people merely going by each other), but it refers to the chess rules' technicality wherein a capture is allowable under an exception to the rules governing the movement of pawns, therefore slightly more complicated and tricky than the usual, simple moves of an apparently insignificant piece. What seems routine and unimportant can become strategic, pivotal, conclusive. Because, increasingly, the only thing that is important is the individual thinking about the self. It is more and more about "me," because of the proliferation of advice, standards, and possibilities of achievement, physical make-up, and emotional well-being. I am likely to be so pre-occupied with myself, and what is right or wrong for me, that I will really not notice the person right next to me, in front of me, paired up with me—the person who might make a move that will affect me. We are so actively thinking, twenty-four/seven/three-sixty-five, that the cartoonist Bruce Eric Kaplan, in the course of an interview with Terry Gross on *Fresh Air*, when it was suggested to him that there could be an activity powerful enough to keep him from thinking while he was doing it, remarked, "Please give me that activity, and I'll take it all day long!"

Trying to avoid thinking one day after another lengthy, provocative interview with Rodgers, I attempted to lose myself in the scores of books in the artist's home. As I turned the pages of a large-format Marlene Dumas book, I chanced upon an excerpt she chose from Jean Genet's *Thief's Journal* (1949) in which the criminal celebrates the crime by exclaiming that while committing the burglary "you don't think." Of course, I couldn't help thinking of the paintings. So many of Rodgers' figures are either thinking too much or committing some cerebral crime that we'll never know about, one that they'll silently suffer for, a trivial crime, with no victim, no evidence, no indictment—only the sentence they impose upon themselves, not to repeat it, but never to forget it, always to be tantalized by the desire they shouldn't be having.

In *En Passant*, among the figures just missing each other because of the burdensome presence of their own self-consciousness, here is the familiar face of another favorite Rodgers model, one he stopped and first photographed on an East Village street. Her nakedness in this scene is especially interesting because Rodgers is perfectly willing to integrate and create bodies and heads as he sees fit. In this case, another model's naked body is seamlessly joined to this gorgeous face. This process suggests the familiar metaphorical saying that so-and-so is so emotionally exposed that they seem "naked" even when fully clothed. (You can see that kind of nakedness at the left edge of the painting, in the young man's face.) Rodgers mixes his nudes with his semi-nudes and his fully-clothed figures, and the effect on the student of his work is that the ideas of clothing and skin, concealment and exposure, are stirred and stewed and synthesized to the point where only the face matters, in terms of the spiritual freight of any given painting. In the arrangements he invents and composes, Rodgers finds a source of infinite human interaction and evasion. "The paintings are in the end constructs of my imagination," he says, "and the characters and settings are just a slightly fantastic amalgam of the exotic variety I encounter every day of my life."

Rodgers loves to look, and he loves to see someone just on the verge of doing something, but at the instant before the action is clear. "Motion or activity of any kind, including even the most simple movement, can momentarily create an illusion of purpose and meaning," he says. He is interested in the more honest moments in between action, when "non-action" could be said to obtain, the difficult-to-abide but fascinating-to-observe gap in between recognizable behaviors. Of course, most of us could probably benefit from directly experiencing more of those moments ourselves, or even whole stretches of actual non-action, which might involve reflection, contemplation, meditation, or even prayer. Rodgers' paintings give us a break, in a sense; they momentarily stop us by making us conscious of how his figures remain forever stopped, and for a little while we can possibly observe our own vectors: where are we pointing, where are we heading, and where are we going? What Rodgers insists in his work is that there may be no true or accurate answer to these questions.

6. Eros and Authenticity

"I am interested in somebody being present to something."
—Terry Rodgers

Rodgers is particularly interested in authentic engagement of any kind, however marginal or mysterious. He cares little about what someone is present to, whether it's a lucid presence or a presence a-swirl in vagueness, as long as there is *something*. Although ideas are vitally important to his work, he places something else ahead of ideas: "My work," he says, "is primarily about looking at us *being*." Sometimes what people look like in their most exposed, unrehearsed, and characteristic moments is not as we think it should be. Overwhelming grief is like that, as is sudden, intense joy. Rodgers involves himself in less extreme, more usual moments. And although he is obviously interested in depicting youth and beauty, and what that represents, he is primarily interested in what he calls "the magic of reality, the unseen parts, as well as what is inappropriate or taboo to view—the un-look-at-able." Rodgers is militantly on guard against "the phony, the pretentious, and the pedantic," and he fights to reveal and banish these human tendencies by dedicating himself to the verities of anatomy, gesture, light, and "the interconnectedness of everything." But that interconnectedness does not imply personal connectedness, only that all the vectors converge and add up and matter in some way. He is drawn to represent vitality as it comes in contact with "realities" and "fictions"; he is interested in young adults because of their "blank slate" being, as he puts it, over which "we can watch the clouds form," he goes on, smiling, mischievously mixing his metaphors. ("As if metaphor is somehow inherently a pure and consistent mode," he adds.) "Maybe we can only know how we're looking at anything," he admits, "or maybe only that we are looking and seeing falsely, despite our best efforts, because our lenses are tinted, and because there are no answers, even though we so badly want there to be answers."

Because of the prominence of attractive young figures in states of undress, and even the occasional fully naked figure, the question of Rodgers' work in relation to eroticism is inevitable. Only the most fundamentalist observers would see any of the pictures as "pornographic," and only *Between Acts* and *The Watchman* would seem likely to provoke such an extreme reaction. Whether Rodgers is, at root, descriptive and documentary, or suggestive and fantastic, is probably as much in the eye of the beholder as whether or not he paints "beauty." At times, he appears to restrain himself; at other times, he goes for broke, rejecting almost every stricture of middle-class morality and conventional sense of beauty. But what he insists on is that we continue to be obsessed with the idea that, like correct answers, something called "perfection" exists, and, not only that, we have a right to it, and we think we could recognize it if we saw it. Paradoxically, Rodgers insists both that "perfection is a lie" and that "the idea of truth is a lie, which means that the idea of a lie is, in some sense, a lie."

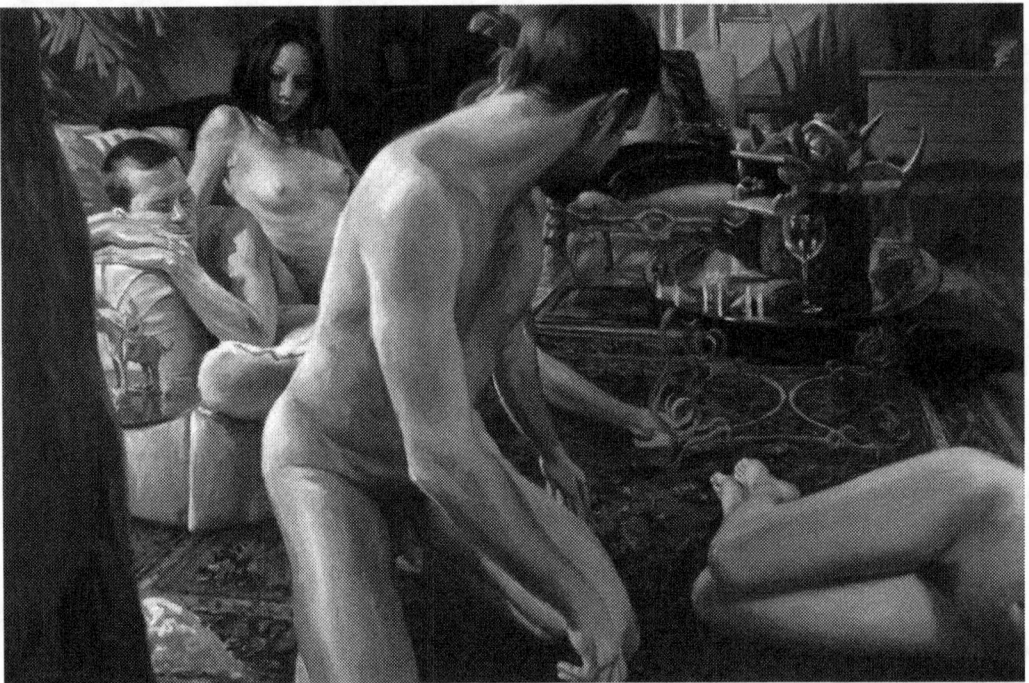

Fig. 41. *Between Acts* (2000, 54" x 84")

In the case of *Between Acts*, Rodgers holds back very little. Everything is exposed, perhaps the worst of desire, or perhaps just the brute essence of it; Rodgers insists he is not taking sides. This is a picture of primal forces in the living room. No doubt this same room has hosted many other ordinary scenes, and how appalled those placid participants would be if they knew about this one! It is all very sinister, foreboding, dark. There is an ape-like movement in the hulking figure in the foreground, and the murky tone, the ennui of the characters on the couch, and the dark unknown on the left all add up to an ominous and threatening side of humanity. The African head on the table is a suburban symbol of some undercurrent of forces we don't usually address and can't understand (or don't want to recognize) in our living rooms.

Unlike some of the other pictures, which are less overtly physical, this painting is raw in its physicality. In most of the other pictures, the viewer's mind jumps to sexual innuendoes; in this one, that's all right out on the table, and what you notice in addition, in particular, are the three other, reposing figures, bored, with no reading of incipient sexual innuendo. What do we do now? But the power still remains in the turn of the figure and the thrust of the dark, the red, and the black. You have the sense that this is what Rodgers really sees in our way of living. What is really going on in all of the civilized and nice places is some kind of masquerade that covers up a primitive, passionate, sinister underside that is the more real side of human consciousness, if not behavior.

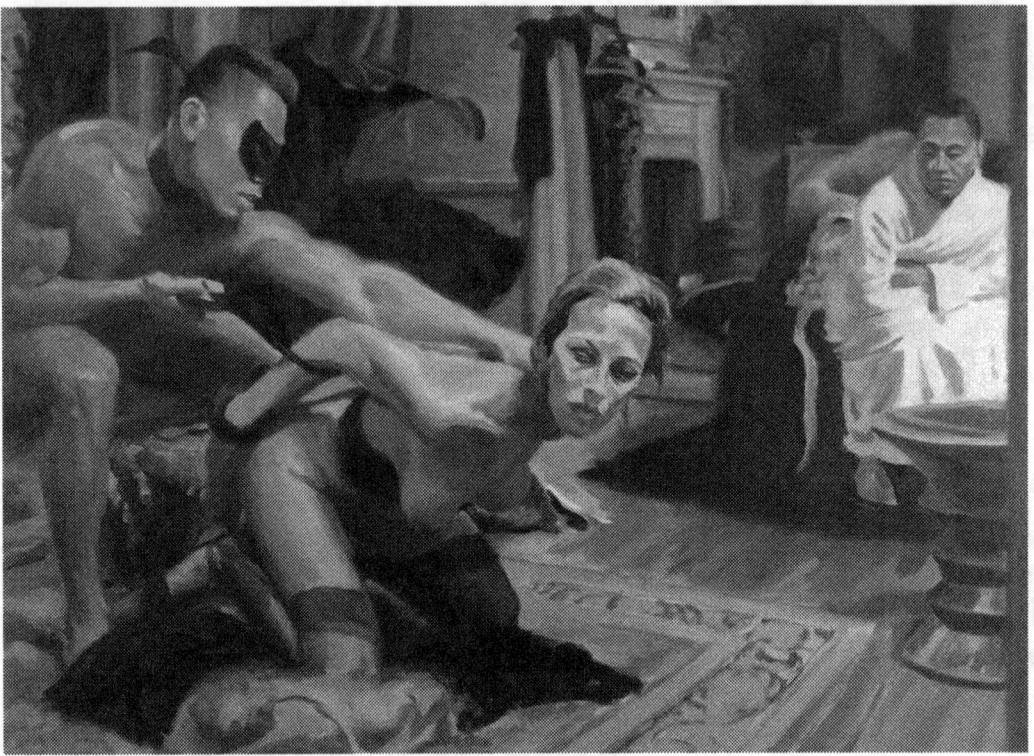

Fig. 42. *The Watchman* (1998, 38" x 54")

The Watchman involves a trio of figures, two engaged in some kind of violent sexual act, and a third one watching. It's a dark scene, murky, and you can't exactly tell what the experience of the two participants is, how much is simply performance (or whether the watcher is instructing, commanding, or merely observing). The watchman himself is stoic, stone-like, unresponsive, unemotional. Perhaps it's a joke about the inscrutable "oriental." There is a sense of despondency, ennui, dissatisfaction about himself—not about them. It's an apparent entertainment, and you don't know whether he's purchased a voyeuristic pleasure or whether the three are acquaintances. His experience is about himself, not about them. Look at all of the vectors: the immediately striking force is the one that pulls the rope, and then there is her apparent resistance, with the gaze of the watchman less forcibly influencing the two of them. The key to the power of the picture is not "the watchman's" outsider status—his palpable outsideness—but his inwardness. He is watching himself. That vector we all have operating all of the time.

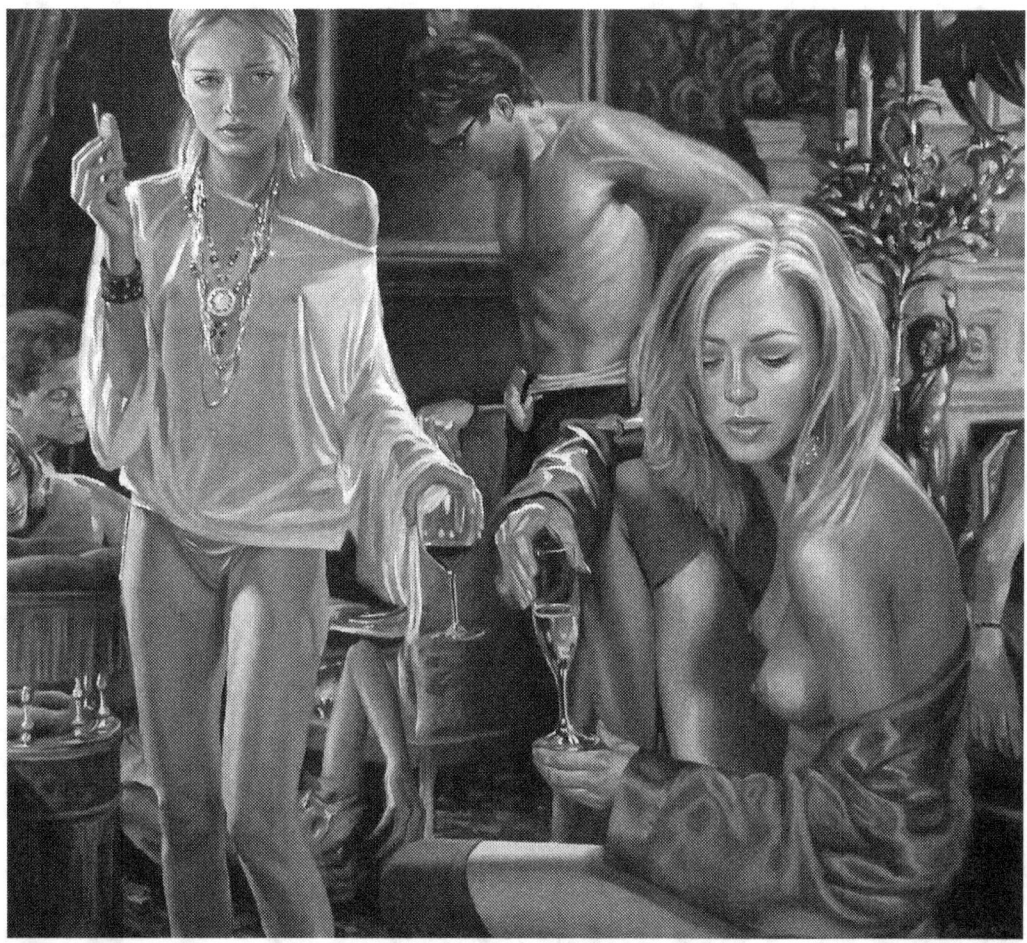

Fig. 43. *Geometries of Innocence* (2003, 48" x 54")

Geometries of Innocence suggests the possibility of authenticity in an unspoiled state, but is it in this painting? The eyes and breasts of the young woman on the left are extremely well-painted, alive with the reality of the human being represented in paint. Her legs are great, too. By holding the glasses so carefully so as not to spill, they show their respect for the ultimate, unchangeable laws of nature. Geometry is about natural law as humans understand it and express it, about angles. The plural—"geometries"—suggests that there may be natural laws we don't yet understand because, as Rodgers observes, "What can they possibly know about the origins of their lives, the past that produced them, that larger context that is so far beyond their comprehension? Of all of this, they remain remarkably innocent."

There is an obvious contrast between old-world elegance and the nouveau youth. We might guess that these "kids" are well off and working in the modeling industry. Born wealthy or not, they are certainly connected, and they're probably too good-looking to simply be a party of rich kids. It is a picture of multiple ideals, icons of certain aspects of our present and past culture. This is one of the series of three paintings (see also *The Night Deck* and *Approximations of Immortality*) in which we can see the evidence of Rodgers having shifted his palette, if temporarily, resulting in effects both harsh and seductive. The purples and violets seem to have taken over from the reds as the dominant tones. It drips sexuality, and the figures seem to flow, too, on the furniture and on the floor.

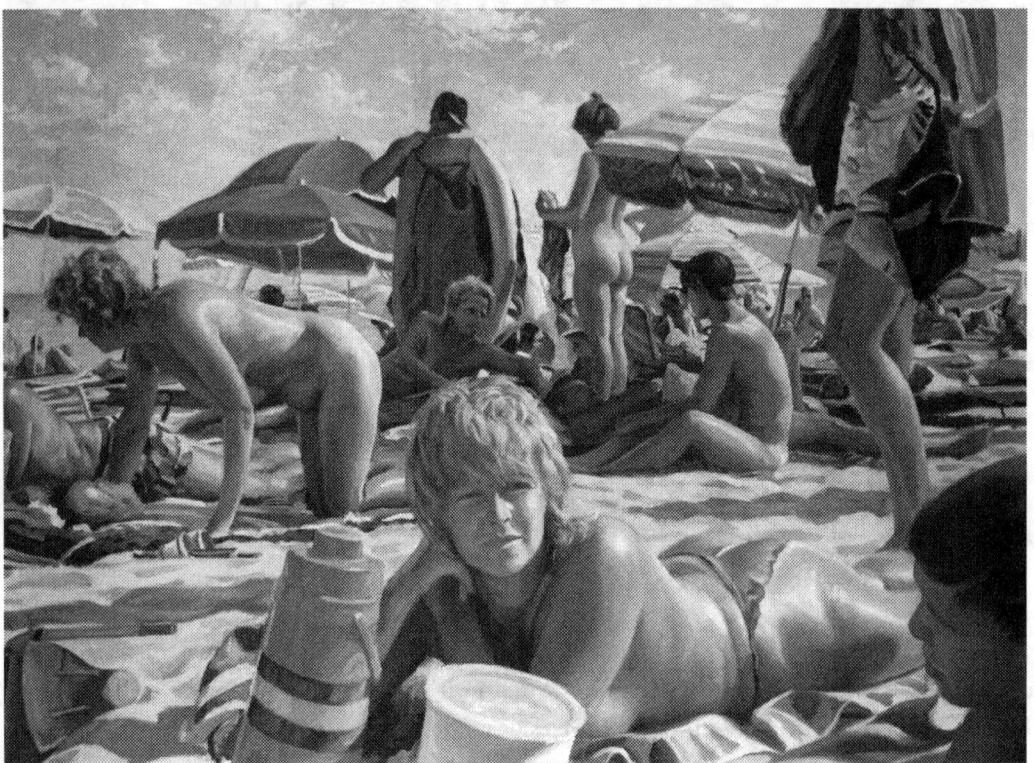

Fig. 44. *The Pink Thermos* (1994, 54" x 76")

The Pink Thermos is a sea of flesh! Your eye floats across these surfaces, across the waves of flesh. There is the guy leaning on his elbow under the umbrella, a small figure. The subtle pull between the absolute normality of being human and physical and that suggestion that somehow there's more to it than that. (Spinoza: our body is everything). The standing headless figure, because of the kind of shadow that he creates, and the unknown that he represents, suggests repression, secrecy, otherness, prurience, voyeurism. Effectively dead center is the banality of the thermos and this questioning, perceiving face that is in no way engaged in subterfuge, that is the embodiment of authenticity, for better or worse. There is so much depth, or dimensionality. Rodgers is inviting us to see the behavioral complexity of the culture, and the degree to which everyone is at risk, one way or another, because of all of the factors that tempt them, drive them, and even indirectly affect them. The experience of the central female figure seems to be expectation, a searching expectation—not upset, but alert, waiting, concerned. She does not know what she's waiting for; her waiting is what the viewer feels as a desire to know.

The women of *Between Acts* and *The Watchman* are at risk in obvious ways. Unlike *Elizabeth*, in the painting of the same name, whose naked self-possession seems convincing, and the female in the foreground of *The Pink Thermos*, who seems thoughtful but unthreatened, many female figures in Rodgers' works do appear at risk because, Rodgers suggests, women have long served as obvious symbols of interior risk. Some are merely used by men, as perhaps the woman in *Rewriting the Book* is used as an inspiration, the basis for a fantasy, or even as a muse by the older man staring at her so pointedly. Few of them appear as damaged or even destroyed as the central figure in *The Exchange*, but the two women in *The Opacity of Light* are representative: something has happened or might happen that bodes ill. The bound woman in *The Watchman* is obviously the most physically vulnerable, but her expectant glance behind seems to indicate a degree of complicity in her apparent victimization.

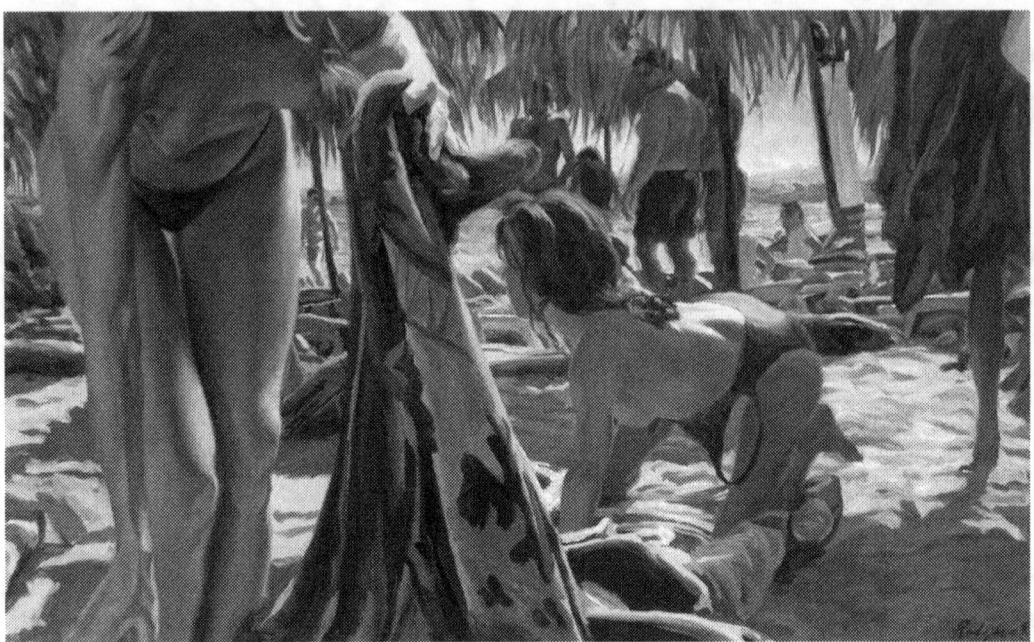

Fig. 45. *Morea* (1996, 60" x 102")

In *Morea*, another endlessly absorbing beach scene, the central female character is very young and seems to be crawling to safety. This beautiful painting is impressive in size, composition, technique, and subject matter. A lesser painter would call it his masterpiece, but for Rodgers, this is just something he does, or something that he could be said to have done back in the twentieth century because the beach paintings have disappeared from the new work and been replaced by interiors. A half-clothed girl is crawling like an animal. One can't tell her age. She could be fourteen, but not eighteen. She seems to be a young, untutored, unspoiled being in the midst of all this older, churning vacation normality. This is a painting about everyday threats hovering at the edge of young people's lives, the ominous side of the quotidian. (Lucy Corin's novel, *Everyday Psychokillers: A History for Girls,* which is set in Florida, presents a sinister literary analogue to this painting.) A central burly figure in the background appears both sinister and relaxed. There is a shroud-like figure at the right, walking, and a woman on the left picking up a towel, who is clearly in the business of doing nothing significant, yet her hovering chest and shadow add another ominous note in the midst of these gentle threats, the fronds and the figures. The younger girl is caught in what clearly seems like a reaction to something unnerving that sets off rhythms of shadows and light, uneasy feelings, and the distant shore across the water is caught and threatened in a sea of light, sunbathers, and sand. What we see in this girl looks like happiness, but she's also a symbol of being caught. Her half-nakedness is natural but slightly underscores an unmistakable vulnerability. Her being partly naked is normal and comfortable and meaningless, and yet in the context of the entrapment of her general condition seems to emphasize her exposure and risk. The adult world is really what's threatening her. Her own looming maturity is not the problem—it's that unidentifiable something else, the man-made world that will intrude on and dominate her nature.

In *The Labyrinth*, the vulnerable female character is all alone, apparently trying to find a way out. In *Apollonian Rhythms*, a formally dressed woman has a very protected arm (her long black glove) but a terribly vulnerable neck and shoulders. *The Definite Article* features a female character who appears to feel like prey in relation to the nearby male. *Buying Time* shows a woman ill at ease in her surroundings, surrounded and trapped. In *Approximations of Immortality*, the half-naked woman with the less than perfectly shaped body feels the pressure of a gaze from behind, and the woman at the lower right in *A Silver Lining* turns to look behind her with at least mild apprehension. In *Sound of the Sea* and *The View*, the women are thinking hard, but about what we can't be sure. *Halloween Breakfast* presents the innocent child most obviously at risk. The two little girls of *And Then There Were None* are also at risk, as are the adolescent girls in *Beach Venus* and *The Deck*.

Some figures are more mysteriously threatened, as the dressing or undressing woman in *The Conversation*. The central figures of *Cross Currents* and *Between Two Worlds* appear trapped (and maybe it's the artist himself, in the self-portrait on the right, whose ideas could threaten the peace of mind of the female figure in the latter case). In *A Sleeping Sense of Life According to Love*, the woman may simply be aware, all of a sudden, that someone nearby is thinking too much about her. The figure on the right in *Geometries of Innocence* is not innocent, but she is also not fully secure and protected. The pensive quality in the face could be regret and foreboding. Similarly, the sophisticated woman with the dog in *The Grammar of Democracy* seems unthreatened but brooding.

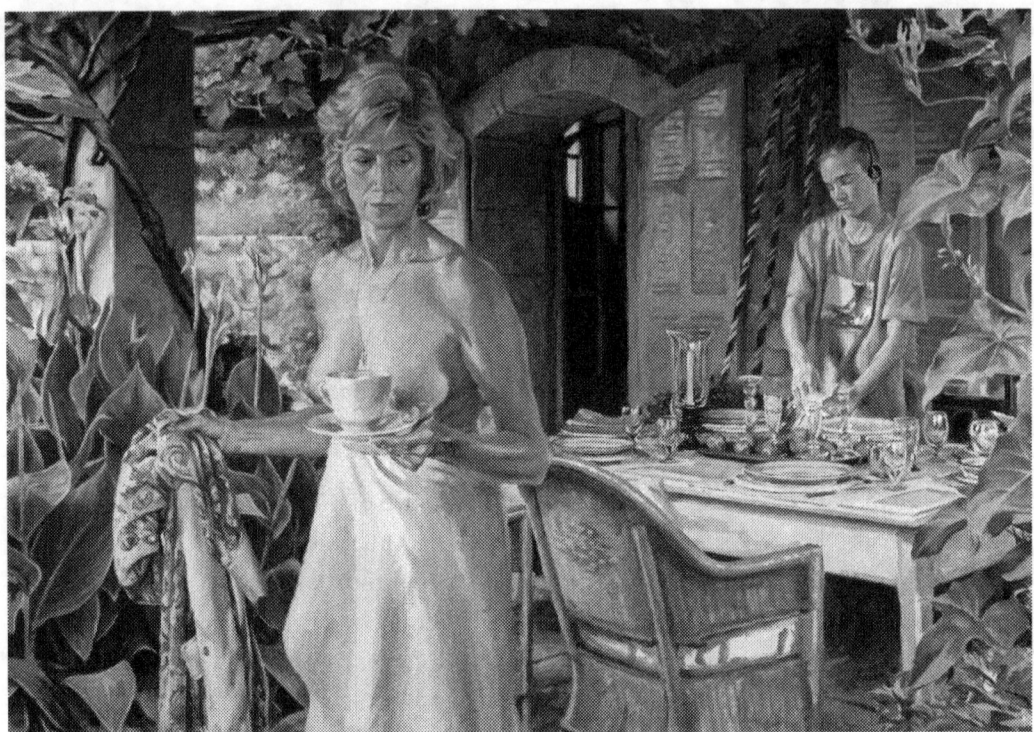

Fig. 46. *Boyz II Men* (1999, 56" x 81 ½")

Occasionally, the innocent in possible emotional or spiritual trouble is a male, as in *Boyz II Men*, *En Passant*, *Hear No Evil*, and *His Collection*. And the man in *Damaged Kingdom* seems to have only the phone as a lifeline to safety. The fully exposed male in *Shades of Olympus* is presented wearing only a watch. Is he at risk or in charge? He is certainly involved in a churning, roiling scene within which he functions perhaps as a counterpart to the dying man in *Timepiece*, a human chronometer, whose aging is inevitable and certain to be fatal. In *Boyz II Men*, which reads like a companion piece to *Hear No Evil*, we see an adolescent boy with a Walkman, probably setting the table but looking like he's playing with toy cars. Painted at the same time and in the same palette as *And Then There Were None* and *Hear No Evil* (really a companion piece to both of them), this gorgeously painted work is just as suggestively sinister. Of course, given the body of Rodgers' work that tempts us toward narrative, it's quite likely that he's inviting the viewer "to make something up," to manufacture meaning, to fabricate plot and character and setting. Are we really wanting to "see" this "older" female figure with her exposed breasts as a threat to the young man, who, given the title, is evidently listening to music of "another culture." Or does the title merely suggest that he has become or will become a man too quickly? Can the cocoon of his suburban culture be unsafe after all? Can dangerous sexuality and the "hear-no-evil" image of the young boy be related to an older woman who might be his grandmother? In fact, of course, we can't know what's in either of their minds. Only in our own. To American suburban viewers, this is at least an anomalous situation, perhaps an unimaginable one. The suggestion that the painter must provide an explanation indicates the state of sexuality in this country. There is a contrast between her light body and towel and the doorway and shadow behind her, and a contrast between the heaviness inside there, this unknown place, and a spectacular sunlit place: we see into the darkness, we see the order of the table and the frequent disorder of what people think and feel.

Rodgers offers an observation about what he sees as he looks back on this work: "It's about all of the stuff that goes through a viewer's mind, all of the stuff that the culture-bound viewer brings to the piece. That and the brushstrokes and palette." In this case, the palette is decorative; the content does not match. Despite the "pretty" colors and lovely represented space, no one could comfortably hang this on the wall of their happy suburban home, where the space and mood that is desired and constructed is serving some vision of "home," which means safety, or the absence of threat, and order, or the absence of confusion. This is one of the great desires that America represents, the single-family-home-as-castle. The American dream of home ownership. But what is in the home; what twisted dreams and shocking nightmares fester there? When does desire turn on itself?

If desire can be anatomized and classified, the desire that is "the best" might well be the desire that is the biggest and can be sustained over years in spite of temporary defeat and ongoing despair (cf. *Timepiece* and *Rewriting the Book*). Or the desire that is the best may be the smallest bit of the desire that can be focused on and accomplished and give satisfaction in the short run. A Napoleon desire or a workman desire. We channel desire into things and processes and persons that will civilize it, control it, take the edge off of it: marriage, jobs, houses, cars, fashion, vacation, children, hobbies. We order and rationalize it because we cannot keep burning with the fine gemlike flame—it rages into a conflagration or is too controlled and sputters out. Repetition and superstition save us from the cuts and burns and aches of desire.

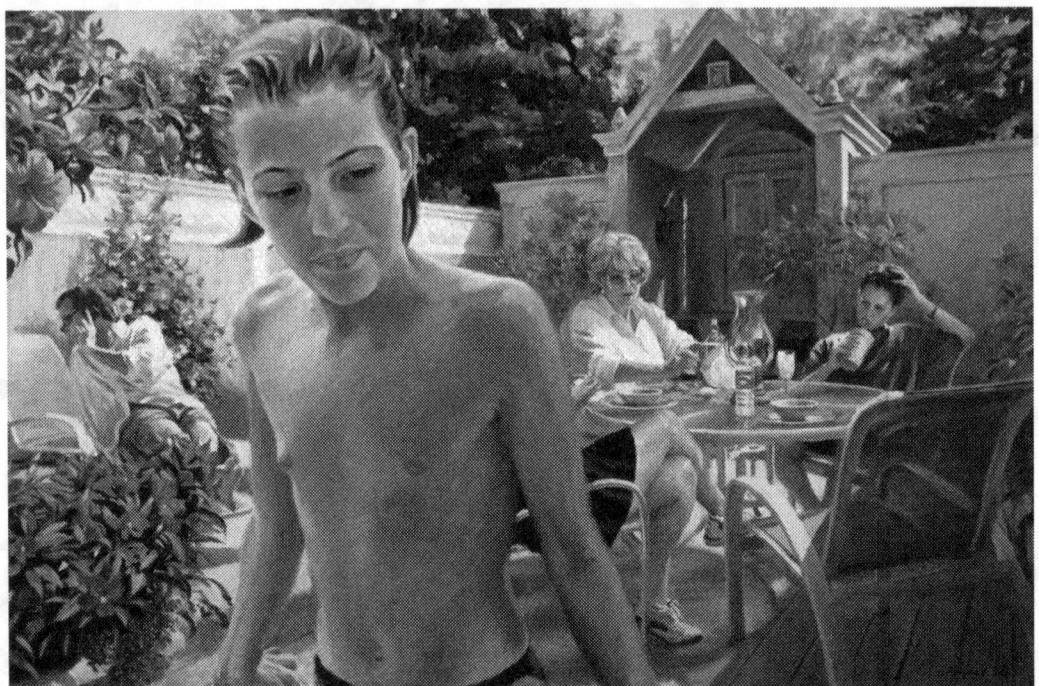

Fig. 47. *The Deck* (1999, 40" x 62")

Sometimes desire comes upon us unawares in the ghostly possibilities of other people's ideas, or the notions floating throughout the entertainment system that is American culture. *The Deck* shows a semi-naked child who seems to be fleeing from the others, all clothed and otherwise engaged. Their relaxed routine is her crisis. This is another of the "decorative" palettes showing action that is anything but decorative. Where this kid is going is in her head, and it's about what's sprouting in the suburbs. Children like her are supposedly protected, but they are in fact subjected to so much, very likely too much. She is young but on the verge of no longer being a child, and her nascent sensuality and budding sexuality perhaps offer a troubling moment of self-awareness. And others are beginning to respond differently to her as well. It is all natural and unnatural within the stylized suburban fiction. They are walled in, walled away, protected, and trapped. Once again, a telephone plays a prominent role; the telephone user is away from the others, oblivious to significant developments close at hand.

We manufacture processes by which we can addictively, compulsively, obsessively inject the energy of desire into something that will be harmless (golf), constructive (work or chores), or redemptive (various religious and charitable enterprises). Save yourself from addiction and obsession by raising the ritualized repetition to a religious status. Desire twists the body and contorts the face, distorts relationships, invents them, confuses things. Desire can inspire or degrade, according to whether or not the feedback is good or bad, as interpreted by the desiring person.

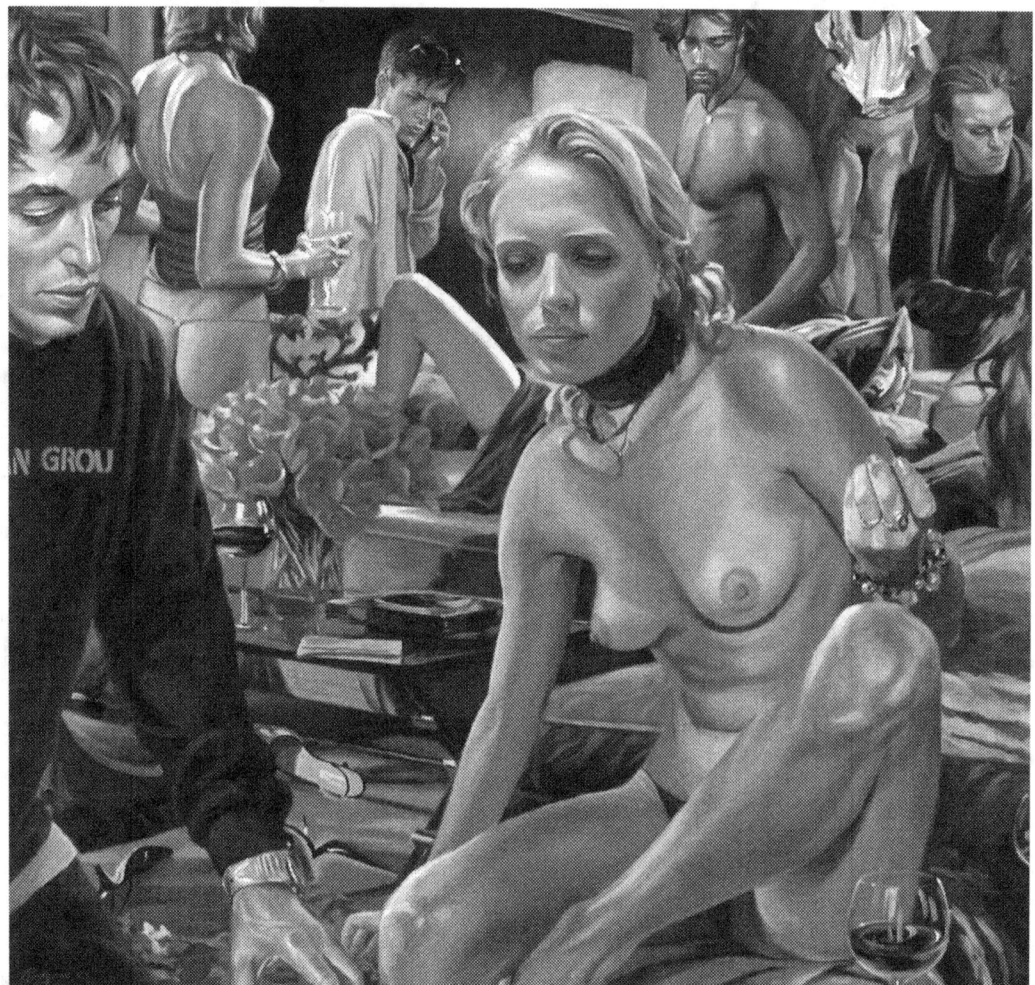

Fig. 48. *All About Eve* (2003, 62" x 66")

In *All About Eve*, the central figure is exposed, but we see very soon that we really can't know "all about her." The model for "Eve" is one of Rodgers' favorite faces. This particular painting features pairings: Eve and the Eric Fischl look-a-like painting on the wall behind her, two exposed women; Eve holding the napkin that echoes the one on the table; and the leg in the center of the picture, which echoes her raised leg. The central male and female characters both seem to be concerned, conscious, alert to something. There is a possible interaction between the two. There is of course the nakedness, which becomes secondary on further viewing, as we become accustomed to all of the light emanating from Eve's skin. The longer you look, the less naked Eve is in her body, and the more naked she is in her mind. There is a contrast between the niceness or smoothness of her chest and the knee and hand. Her mental state is somewhere between that of the chest and that of the knee and hand. Her chest has pale to darker skin that is almost like an icon, almost like an idea of something "nice." But the knee and hand are more cartilaginous, more real. The chest looks less and less real the more you look at it, but the knee is completely real. Back and forth, back and forth goes the interplay. Then there is the reversal in the art of the naked bottom and covered top over her left shoulder, the take-off on the Fischl. The Blue Man Group T-shirt suggests that this group of four men could be "blue." Shoes have been tossed on the floor. The poppies are intense red. Reds and skin tones: the rhythms of the flesh, but cerebral rather than sexual. The napkin on the table is a work of art all by itself. It is a pure abstraction, painted beautifully, seven or eight inches long and two inches or so high. It shimmers in the center of the painting, like a narrow window to another world.

When asked about the significance of Eve's nudity, Rodgers says simply, "She only *happens* to be naked. Everybody thought sex was the solution, and everybody jumps to the conclusion that nakedness is correlated with sex, but often that's not the case. It appears that getting undressed didn't get her what she was looking for. Sex is only one part of being human, and nakedness is another, and they can be experienced separately, and neither one of them guarantees pleasure or satisfaction."

After awhile, one notices the intensity of the facial expressions. Eve's physicality is about her mind, not her sexuality. Her posture is about balancing her momentary mental state, not about sexual exposure or expression. What we often forget is that the place between decisions is the worst, that indecision preys on the mind as much as being out of control, or at someone else's mercy, or waiting by the phone does. What we can see once we take our cultural blinders off is a wonderful portrait of a fragile and vulnerable, yet strong human being. But those blinders are hard to remove, and the dynamic here is once again a favorite of Rodgers', that vectoral push-and-pull that is both between directions and concepts. Everything is really so much more complicated than we give ourselves time to realize. Francine Prose, writing in *The Wall Street Journal*, alluded to this problem in a phrase when she referred to "our vapid notions of gender, romance and sexuality." Rodgers thrives on the complexities of nature, humanity, and the infinite relations within these separate but connected worlds. "That art which displays the most difficulties will be the most agreeable and, consequently, the most intellectual," wrote El Greco in a marginal note in his edition of Vitruvius's *On Architecture*. Rodgers is difficult, in the end, because he refuses to bow to the possible concerns, proprieties, and sensitivities of various political and moral forces. He is "in your face" with the carefully painted breast that calls attention to itself as both simply a breast and also as a cultural icon that is increasingly the vehicle for high-end advertising. The difficulties Rodgers "displays" are the unresolved confusions of our own personal unfinished business, both moral and intellectual.

Where you are—psychically and geographically, socially and intellectually—limits you to who and how you are. The tendency to believe that now, more than at any other time in history, one can "have it all," is a destructive tendency. It ignores the syndrome of expecting everything and being swamped by too many choices, too many people, and too many possibilities. There is no way to discriminate among them, to order them—no reliable point of reference. So where are Rodgers' people? Stuck in between, as often as not. Their "where" indicates the contingencies of who and how they are, and many seem, understandably and authentically, confused to the point of paralysis by their world. They have no way of getting their bearings in a time and place in their lives where they probably arrived with the expectation that there they could have everything desirable.

To be present is traditionally seen as a good thing. But now we are both too present and too absent because of the capacities of computers and cell phones, of email and text messages and voicemail. The presence and absence is intensifying. Where in fact are our thoughts residing; where are our feelings grounded? The body is visible, but the mind is no longer certain to follow it. Rather than a fortification to protect us, the body has become a flimsy façade, and one that poorly hides the obvious fact that we don't know how to be wholeheartedly present to anything or anyone. Our consciousness is disseminated, diffused, and scattered. And this phenomenon can be exacerbated by the promotions of certain kinds of people—models, or super-models—which sends us a riveting message: that we don't have to settle for people who look less appealing than those stunning models. Rodgers is able to have it both ways because of his use of beautiful young people in his paintings; he galvanizes the viewer's attention even as he draws attention to our cultural habit of privileging the surfaces of things.

Writers like Lionel Trilling and Rollo May have traced the connection between eros and authenticity in interesting ways. Rodgers simplifies what they have elaborated upon by clearly indicating the degree to which our erotic sincerity is the shortest route to authentic perception, feeling, and action. Not perhaps the best strategy for living, but the most palpably direct and honest gauge of being. Rodgers inspires models to pose in such a way as to be present and authentic to something in their characters and conditions at the moment he takes their pictures, and more often than not there is an erotic aspect or tone to the pose that results. He manages to alert them to something, and then he combines their separate alertnesses in ways that multiply the vectors and the possibilities to create a synergy that lends mystery to his compositions. The girl is not only setting the glass down, but something else is also going on. There is a simultaneity of genuine gesture and presence of being, a synchronicity of physicality and spirituality that one doesn't at first glance get.

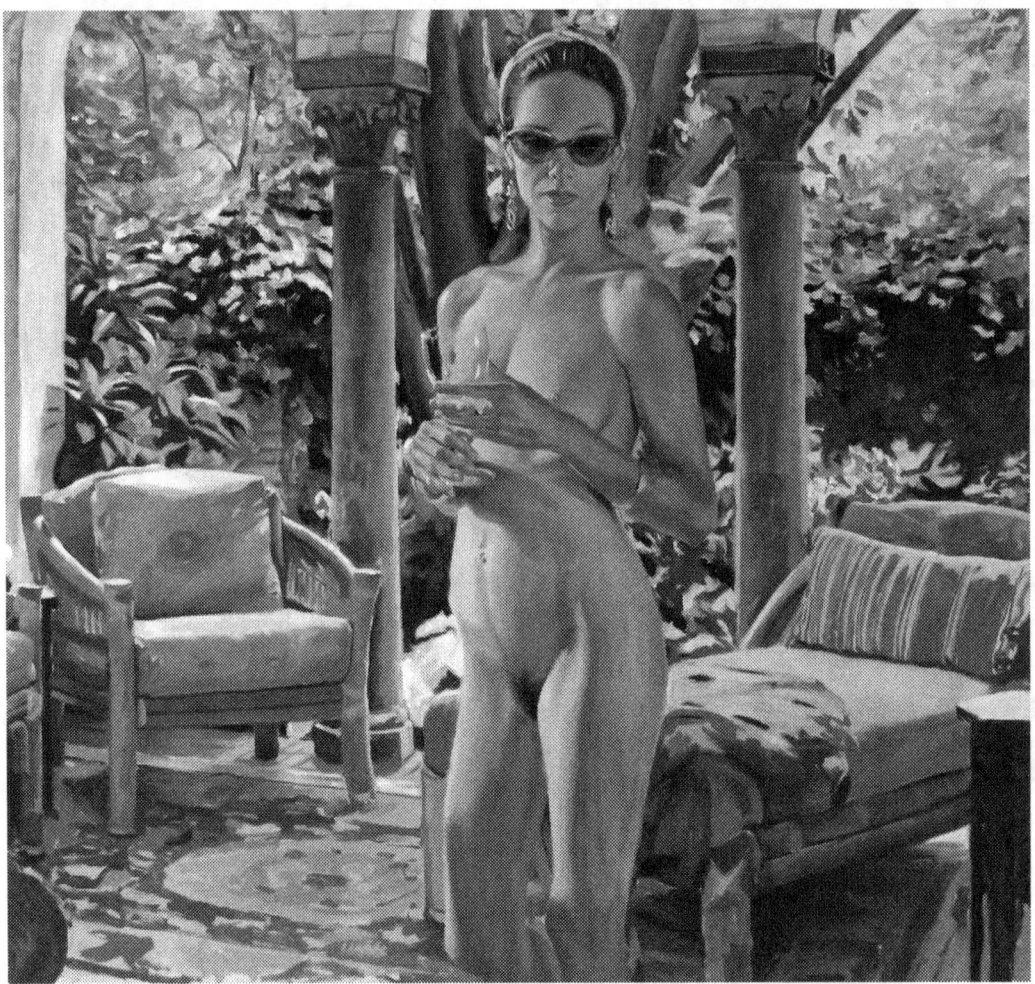

Fig. 49. *The Art of Living* (2003, 60" x 65")

The Art of Living features a completely exposed and yet mysterious woman in one of Rodgers' single-figure paintings. She is sleek and aerodynamic like some kind of vehicle. And thus, seen in one way, she is artificial, hardly human, just another part of the very "contemporary" environment, which seems to be a suburban backyard with some kind of wall and forestry between this and the next house or subdivision. It could be southern or northern. In the context of a very contemporary and truly suburban world, we are presented with a person who is completely disguised merely by having her eyes hidden behind sunglasses. And yet you have the wonderful sense of her not being disguised because she's naked. We see the flesh of arms, thighs, hips, and the tonalities of the paint. Rodgers has painted her so that in seeing the flesh you see her, not an artificial image. The skin of her hip is like revelation. It's about seeing her being. In the flesh of her arm, we sense that we see into her. The human part of her will assert itself even in a world of the most superficial artifice. This is the woman as she really is, in her skin, but perhaps she doesn't know what she is.

Like Renaissance paintings of the angel announcing the coming birth of Jesus, there is a radiance here, and everything disappears into the upper right. The chair is smacked with light. This is a place glowing with some presence. It is as if there is an event, a coming down to mortality—a very real presence of being human, of being flesh. Her flesh is mortal, fragile, and vulnerable: suntanned lower legs, private parts pale. Arms tanned, face tanned. This is what it is to be human, flesh and blood, bound in that human form, and how it is experienced in and by her body. We're all victims of someone else's desires or our own. And getting what we want is not necessarily the answer (one thinks of Shaw's "two tragedies in life," not getting what we want or getting it.) Unsatisfied desire is at least a tonic, a motivation, a goad. If we can keep it free—independent of mere formality, habit, formula, routine—it can seem to sustain us. Desire, at its best, inspires alertness and a lively sensitivity. And joy? Where do we find it in Rodgers' paintings? In the painting itself, in the connections, the interwoven complexity, and in the way he embraces life as he finds it, seeing us for who we are, transforming his vision into painting after glorious painting.

7. Inconclusive

"I'm always ready to go on to the next picture."
—Terry Rodgers

Perhaps the most powerful desires are in fact never satisfied. They mutate and evolve, sending their arrows further afield to more distant, less accessible targets, destinations guaranteed not to disappoint desire. More often than not, when our desire comes to an end, it has been abolished only by a destruction so terrible that we regret the success of our quest. Until then, we live for and by desire, and all of the vectoral forces from inside and out. In lieu of better forces and acts, we'll take cell phone and email messages, instant communication, distant, mostly-simulated connection, and, perhaps most powerfully, the inward-pointing fantasies that rain down on us all day long through advertising and entertainment. Not that Rodgers has a solution. He just likes to look at us looking, and looking, and looking, as we turn our arrows on ourselves. We suffer. We bleed. We die. Or we thrive as a sub-set of the circus clown, juggling various incompatible ideas and activities, smiling our way to a cheerful, pleasant, famous oblivion, as in the case of the lately-mourned President Reagan, or, more consciously, in the celebrated Gerhard Richter, whose MOMA retrospective in 2002 featured the theme that he had "not one idea or style, but many." We have to hold many ideas in mind simultaneously, and employ many styles, in order to function on a daily basis.

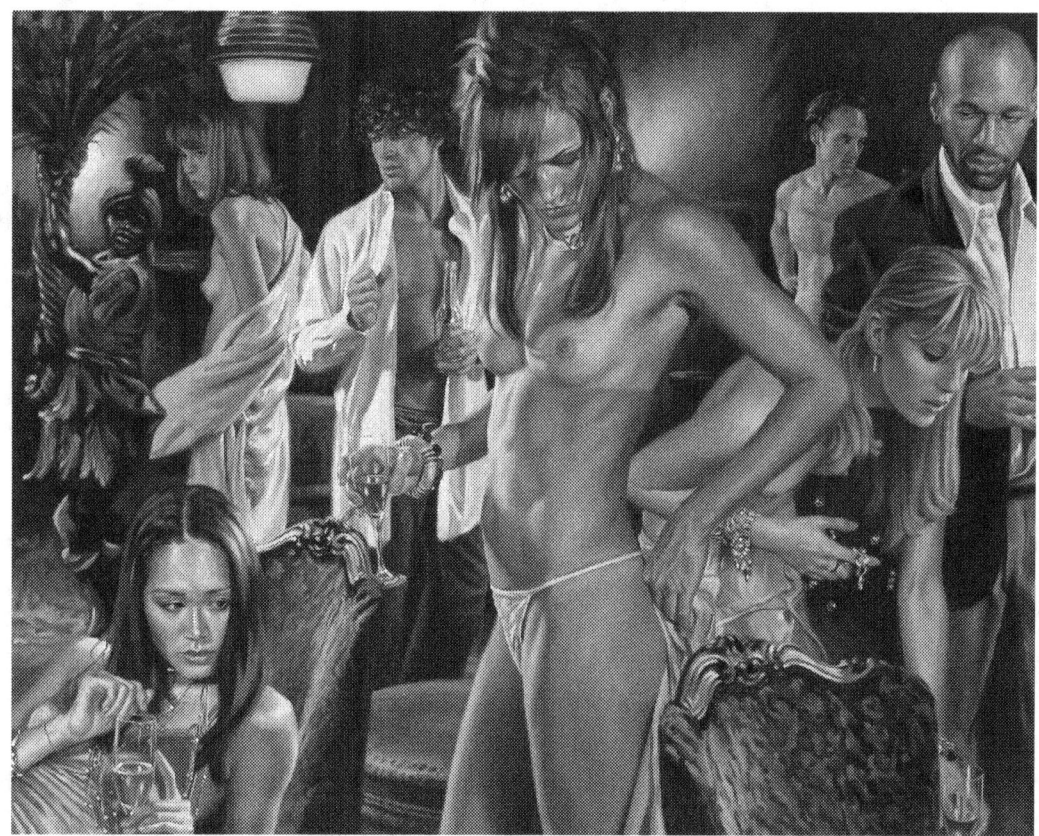

Fig. 50. *Just Like the Night* (56" x 72")

In *Just Like the Night*, Rodgers presents a stunning female nude as the central figure, solid and gorgeous as an oak tree, but after the first thrill of the beauty of the overall arrangement passes, what arrests us is her hand, an extraordinarily well-rendered piece of painting in itself that finally carries more human reality in it than some entire collections of paintings do. Because the woman in the center of painting has her head down, we are thwarted in our mind-reading and story-making. Instead, we resort to her hand to see her humanity and character, in the raised veins and the strength of her grip. The archaic, dark slave artifact in the left background accentuates her freedom and her living presence, but we can not fathom what is going on in this representation of the cliché of a cool club, perhaps downstairs, dark and smoky and full of people from who-knows-where. Yet her voluntary, celebratory nakedness glows with mysterious purpose, and the scene is presented as a *non sequitur*, except that her hand speaks of power, possibility, the improbability of our spectacular existence, and, above all, human touch. We may be without a clue, adrift, and desperate for direction, but we have this sensational core to come back to.

The owner of the Torch Gallery in Amsterdam, Adriaan van der Have, with a major Rodgers show in late 2004, speaks of the "emptiness" that people have to deal with in the twenty-first century, perhaps particularly in America. From a European perspective, he observes, Rodgers' work evokes "the Roman Empire and its bacchanal parties." He believes that Rodgers has received more attention in Europe because "Americans are too close to the situation" to allow themselves to fully participate in the paintings, and that the American art market is more commercial, while Europeans, like himself, show what they feel personally drawn to.

An American curator who has embraced Rodgers' vision, Scope's Robert Curcio, observes, "There are so many different levels in his paintings. You can get lost in the layers and layers of paint and meaning. Rodgers is a strong, serious painter, and you have to work through every painting to get to the point at which it begins to involve you, whether you like to read the clues and build a story or just enjoy the highly designed construction. I love how subtle everything is."

Terry Rodgers, a protean artist capable of producing in any style and of entertaining any idea, continues to chart the vectors of desire with a commitment to a vision that matters. He does not dabble in style nor does he reduce his art to a marketable brand, but he continues to evolve his vision of the introverts and extroverts, the saints and satyrs, the hermits and party animals, living among us, all of them on the surface appearing civilized and socialized, and all of them homogenized by our dulled vision. Rodgers has committed himself to the struggle to show and to see and to think.

Ultimately, the way the vectors in Rodgers' paintings add up is this: they point inward. You can see it in the way he paints the eyes, the foreheads, the inward-turning faces. You can see it in the tentativeness of the postures and gestures. You can see it in the surfaces of the paintings, in the brushstrokes themselves. The vectors are aimed at the mind and heart—and at the soul. But the minds and hearts doubt the existence and location of the soul. As the twenty-first century begins, the vectors point inward as they always have, but they also point right out from the canvas and take direct aim at the viewer. They raise, resist, and fortify our priorities, whether it be merely desire for more material stuff, or desire for so-called "better" things: peace of mind, undisturbed conscience, freedom from anxiety, if not absolute certainty or a perfect faith. That's what Terry Rodgers' work does; it disturbs us, "just like the night"; "Ain't it just like the night," Dylan sings, "to play tricks when you're tryin' to be so quiet?" Rodgers' days and nights, his interiors and exteriors, his clothed and unclothed figures all rattle us. His work unsettles, disrupts, and challenges our carefully orchestrated, endlessly micro-managed nexus of compromise, in this cognitive and strategic age we must negotiate. These paintings ask us to surrender everything and start from scratch, to look at everything as if it is being born before our eyes, ridiculously, extravagantly, and altogether improbably. It's really refreshing, as it turns out, a sense-cleansing relief that we had no reason to expect and could never purchase, but one that we can accept as a generous, authentic gift of human spirit.

Having first seen Rodgers' work in 1994, I made a note to myself: "I can't wait to see what this man will paint in the next few years." Having seen what he's done in the span of a decade, and having assured myself that there is no living artist more capable or more at the peak of his powers, I'm even more eager to see what the next ten years will bring.

Acknowledgements

I owe my interest in painting to Laura Yoder, an interest that was reinforced through the years in the creative work of Janet Robbins, Stephen Zoog, John Zimmerman, Laurie Zimmerman, and Richard Horst. I couldn't have considered this project without generous help from Terry Rodgers himself, especially his cheerful willingness to answer innumerable questions, and the encouragement and assistance of his wife, Estelle Rodgers, a wonderful artist in her own right, whose www.terryrodgers.com website is a treasure for anyone interested in Rodgers and his work. Thanks to Bob Glamb for lending me his house and his research expertise. Annette Federico, whose work I admire, offered valuable advice on an early draft and accompanied me to many museums. Traci Pipkins' support was vital, and she tirelessly reviewed drafts and provided organizational and editorial insights. Jack Z. and Steve J. helped with the international perspective. C.B. kept me going. Thanks to Computer Chip Brown for his technical support and Lori Tolbert for her administrative support. And Joe, as usual, inspired me. As always, this is for Jeanne Louise.—JZ

0-595-32884-9

www.ingramcontent.com/pod-product-compliance
Lightning Source LLC
Chambersburg PA
CBHW081150180526
45170CB00006B/2017